the PeoplePACT®

Achieving Exemplary Performance through Humane Leadership

the PeoplePACT®

Achieving Exemplary Performance through Humane Leadership

By Denise McNerney and Lynn Rolston

Proof that **"BOSS"** can be
more than a four-letter word

green press
INITIATIVE

ISBN 978-1-58597-440-5
Library of Congress Control Number: 2007939458

LEATHERS PUBLISHING
4500 College Boulevard
Overland Park, Kansas 66211
888-888-7696
www.leatherspublishing.com

Dedication

To all of our family and friends, as well as all those who have crossed our paths along the way, as all of you have helped to bring us to where we are today—a place in which we are truly grateful.

DM & LR

Table of Contents

INTRODUCTION

"The best way to predict the future is to create it."

— Peter Drucker

When I was a kid, my dad was the sole breadwinner in the family. He had a college degree and worked in aerospace in California. When I was about 10, my father started coming home at night upset, frustrated and angry about how he was treated by his new boss.

In retrospect, I can see now that my father's boss was a classic micromanager. Constantly asking for reports to explain how each part of a job was done, frequently checking work that was routine and making corrections on every report, all within earshot of other people. She played favorites. "I just can't win," Dad told us. During the years he worked for her he developed health problems that nearly cut short his career.

This work situation had a big impact on our family. I felt like I had lost my "real" father. Instead of the boisterous talking and joking that characterized our dinner table "before her," we were now quiet and anxious.

Years later, after I had worked for good bosses and bad ones, when I had a family around my own dinner table, I wondered: how many employees—and their families—had to endure the destructive effects of bad bossing? Why did so many ineffective, insecure bosses seem blind to the problems they caused for their employees and, ultimately, their companies? Most of all, how could we all do things differently?

— Lynn Rolston, co-author
The People*PACT*

They are uncommunicative about their expectations but don't hesitate to express their anger—loudly—or even publicly. They consider employees expendable and use intimidation as a management tool. Their unrealistic demands undermine family life, jeopardize marriages, and stress the health of those who struggle to please them. These bad bosses—who adhere to a management model that has more to do with power than leadership—have become the biggest obstacle in their company's, and their own, success.

According to a Gallup Organization survey of over 1 million employees (Buckingham, 1999), difficult bosses are the overwhelming reason good workers quit their jobs. At a time characterized by the pared-down, bare-bones corporation, managers can hardly afford to lose the dedicated and experienced workers. And in an increasingly unstable economy, bosses need to see that the path to corporate growth, creativity and productivity is dependent upon the support and input of a creative, productive staff.

The People*PACT* culls the forefront of current thinking to forge a new, mutually satisfying dynamic between bosses and their most important asset: their people. To achieve exemplary performance, it is critical that bosses' focus on *supporting* the performance of their people, rather than on *managing* it. Making and keeping the *PACT* is a highly effective and easy to learn process by which to do this!

The High Cost of "Bossy" Bossing

Nobody really sets out to be the kind of a manager who withholds direction, delegates stress—or simply generates confusion. Most of today's managers were weaned on the authoritarian model—the kind of "Right or wrong, I'm-the-boss" approach that came to prominence during the industrial revolution. Although every manager develops his or her own interpretation of leadership from the democratic to the despotic, accepted models die hard. The distancing strategies some bosses rely on to establish authority can also isolate them from their staff. A cookie-cutter approach to management can make life miserable for the talented employees a boss needs most. The "people skills" they picked up from a command and control type manager can, years later, seem repressive, outdated or even unhealthy for valued staff, the department and even the company. Now, more than ever, the effects of these archaic, shortsighted methods can hit "bossy bosses" where it hurts most: in the bottom line.

Businesses need a new, people-friendly paradigm. This is not only evident in the thousands of companies where meetings are characterized by silence, where CYA memos proliferate while valuable opinions go unexpressed, but in current research, as well. According to a recent survey by Bob Rosner (2001), the author of *The Bosses' Survival Guide* and *"Working Wounded"* columnist, 80% of all bosses squelched their employees input, thwarted their chances for advancement, micromanaged, mismanaged, or simply created problems for their people. Goleman et al (2002, p. 95) provide data that clarifies the situation further. They summarize a Hay Group 2001 analysis of 787 people in a wide variety of organizations, with positions ranging from low to high levels:

> High-level executives and managers, compared with those in the lower rungs, were more likely to rate themselves more generously on twenty EI (Emotional Intelligence) competencies than others rated those leaders on the same competencies...The higher leaders were in an organization, the greater the inflation rate...Those at the highest levels had the least accurate view...

The situation is clear: if the overwhelming majority of workers report significant dissatisfaction with their bosses while bosses remain content with their performance, then dissatisfaction on both sides will continue to grow. If questionable management is the number one reason for employee attrition and there is no stopgap in place to prevent continued flight, then high turnover, skyrocketing retraining costs, and widespread employee dissatisfaction causing low productivity will continue to plague a large segment of businesses. Even in the case of successful companies, one wonders: how much more successful could those businesses be with better bossing and better *Performance Support*?

A New, People-Friendly Approach

Ask a lot of bosses what would make his/her life easier and you are likely to hear answers like this:

"People who see beyond the next paycheck and go the extra mile."

"A room full of self-starters—and strong finishers! People who are tuned-in enough to see what needs to be done and motivated enough to do it."

"Ten team players."

Now ask the men and women who work for those bosses what kind of environment would make them more fulfilled, productive employees and you might hear responses like these:

"A clear idea of what I'm expected to do!"

"All I really want is credit where credit is due. Is that unrealistic?"

"A boss who will support my growth and professional development."

It is in every boss's best interest to find out what the people who work for him/her want. Virtually every employee at every level wants to know what his or her boss wants. But how do you begin to bridge the inevitable power gap that isolates both the boss and the bossed in the traditional office relationship? **The People*PACT* is an actual *PACT*, agreed to by both boss and employee, through which managers and team members identify, define and create the environment that enables them to be their best.**

At its simplest, The People*PACT* is about:

PEOPLE and their contributions are the core of any business. The *PACT* is the process of creating a mutual commitment that aligns employees with organizational goals and leaders with employee's goals.

Furthermore, when leaders incorporate the following principles into ongoing *Performance Support*, individuals and organizations can experience unprecedented success:

Perspective: helping people understand how their contribution and performance fits into and supports the larger picture.

Acknowledgement: building a positive environment supporting growth, development and self-motivation.

Collaboration: maximizing innovation and performance through enhancing communication, mutual support and synergistic teams.

Trust: building the foundation for a thriving work environment that achieves exemplary results.

This book reveals how workers and bosses at every level can create the win-win workplace: an organization that is as positive for employees as it is for bosses and the company as a whole. The People*PACT* outlines the strategies visionary bosses can use to negotiate an equitable and practical workplan for people on every rung of the corporate ladder. And with step-by-step guidance to enhance every team in every business climate, this breakthrough book bridges the gap between bosses and those who work for them by providing a practical, inspiring framework for supportive, respectful leadership and *Performance Support.*

Based upon a **real** *PACT*, drawn from the authors' own proven-successful model and process, The People*PACT* makes managers and employees allies in the ongoing creation of a meaningful, high-performing work experience.

In this transformative book, managers will learn:

- How to set up the *PACT* in their own company to ensure the alignment of personal and organizational goals, reduce conflict and maximize motivation at every level!
- How to use the *PACT* to create a truly collaborative team—from the day of hire onward.
- Strategies for maintaining honest, open communication around job performance.
- Practices to build trust—even in a company that has been run like an "armed camp."
- How to be a leader towards great performance.
- Hands-on techniques for maximizing the potential of their most inventive, resilient, powerful resource: people.
- The secrets to being and staying a supportive boss— even in difficult times.

- What type of acknowledgement gets employees to step up and be their best.

How to Use This Book

The book divides itself naturally into three diagnostic and instructional sections:

Section 1: Chapters 1, 2, 3 and 4. These four chapters focus on making and keeping The *PACT*. This section deals specifically with the *PACT* itself. Readers learn how to:
- Create and adapt The People*PACT* to their department's unique needs.
- Maintain a consistently humane approach through the challenges that are apt to occur over time, including firings, lay offs, relocations, mergers and the like.

Section 2: Chapters 5, 6, 7 and 8 cover the four core principles of humane leadership: Perspective, Acknowledgement, Collaboration and Trust.

Perspective: Every transformation begins with a new perspective. In this chapter, managers are given an understanding of how the principles of humane leadership can enrich their lives—and profit their organizations. They will learn:
- How the authoritarian bossing style evolved;
- The critical difference between leadership and bossing;

- How managers can reach their goals by bringing their life values with them to the office;
- How by bringing the big-picture perspective to frontline workers, the boss can create alignment, facilitate decision-making, totally energize a team and attain the organization's goals.

Acknowledgement. Sincere, specific acknowledgement is a true foundation of the People*PACT*. In these chapters, business leaders learn how to:

- Use clear, targeted verbal and nonverbal cues to mold a cohesive, creative team;
- When to acknowledge and when to hold back;
- How to give positive, powerful *Performance Support* rather than criticism;
- Ways to solicit employees' honest feedback on their performance.

Collaboration: This chapter gets to the heart of building and maintaining an inclusive, collaborative team. Among the topics covered are:

- What departmental meetings can tell about the collaborative condition of the team;
- How to bring the People*PACT* strategies into the hiring process to build cooperation from day one;
- How to overcome collaboration-busters like gossiping, envy and competition;
- How to turn every interaction into a win-win-win situation.

Trust: Cutbacks, diminishing raises, evaporating benefits as well as recent scandals have made workers more distrustful than ever of their bosses and of organizations where they work. This chapter demonstrates how savvy bosses can use the *PACT* to create an atmosphere of trust even in a difficult environment. Readers will learn:
  • How humane truth-telling can build trust;
  • How to be courageous and tell one's truth in a way that leads to greater trust;
  • How to build accountability within the ranks through greater transparency.

Section 3: Chapter 9 helps readers pull it all together including:
  • A summary of the key steps and concepts in making the *PACT*;
  • An outline and format for applying the People*PACT* principles to the *Performance Support* process.

Filled with real-life anecdotes from the front-lines of corporate life, drawn from a combined fifty years of hands-on, innovative leadership, The People*PACT* is an exciting new paradigm for business and a practical method for on-going employee *Performance Support* that will strengthen the team and the prosperity of the company, as well as individual success.

Chapter 1

THE ROAD TO BOSSING WELL

"Management is about arranging and telling. Leadership is about nurturing and enhancing."

— Tom Peters

Why *Performance Support* is Critical

An aspiring leader and consummate team player, Diane spent years searching for methods to improve her ability to manage, direct and contribute to success. Her career mattered to her in profound ways: she could feel its impact in every area of her life. To become a successful, happy person, she knew that she needed to feel fulfilled in her work as well as her personal life. Though they didn't know it, or couldn't articulate it, Diane, her boss, and those she managed, were all searching for The PACT.

Think about the best boss you ever had.
Now think about the worst boss you ever had.

Consider how differently each of these people affected your life, both at work and outside of the office.

Once you have in your mind a vivid image of these two people, return to both of those times in your life and answer the following questions:

When at Work...

- Did you enjoy going to work every day, or was it drudgery?
- Did you seek your boss out for advice and support, or were you on pins and needles whenever he or she was around?
- How did the different bosses affect the quality and quantity of your work? What about the work of your coworkers?
- What was the turnover rate with the different bosses?

After Work...

- What was the tenor of your after-work conversations?
- What was the tone and content of your dinner table conversations with your family?
- How much did each boss affect your mood at home?
- Did you spend your Sunday afternoons dreading Monday morning, or were you able to relax, knowing that all would be well when you returned to the office?

This book is about helping you become that boss you remember as your best—the kind that produces great results while helping employees grow and succeed in their careers. By using the People*PACT* process described in this book, you can engage and support your team members, making them more productive, positive-minded, and ultimately more fulfilled, while simultaneously maximizing performance.

What Gives Bosses a Bad Name?

We know all bosses are not great, but why not? What does it take to be great? Elements of the following story may be all too familiar to many of you as you think about your history with bosses.

> *Diane was a member of the regional executive leadership team of a national healthcare organization—Health Assurance, Inc. Her boss, Murray, started with the company right out of college and worked his way up "through the ranks," as he was fond of reminding anyone who would listen of that accomplishment. Murray summed up his management philosophy in one sentence: "Never trust anyone until they prove themselves to be trust-worthy—then still keep them at arm's length." Before college Murray had served in the military as a drill sergeant. He fondly described his key leader role model there as a "kick ass and take no prisoners" kind of leader. It seemed to his staff that the domineering leadership style he used with them was a direct carry-over from this military experience.*
>
> *Diane became very familiar with Murray's "my-way-or-the-highway" approach. Once, when she was having difficulty scheduling an employee-training program, she turned to Murray for guidance. He advised her to ignore the team's preference and schedule the meeting over a weekend. As he put it, "I have control over my employees' time. They will do what I tell them*

to do." Most of the time, they did. Murray was a large man who frequently raised his voice. He hovered over his employees as he barked orders, and quite often, criticisms. To Diane, Murray was a volcano perpetually on the verge of eruption.

Bad Bossing Isn't Intentional

Bad bossing may be common, but it is rarely intentional. In our example above, Murray did not wake up that morning and think, "How can I make Diane miserable today?" However, in his effort to be what he perceived to be a "strong effective boss," he accomplished just that.

Although some workers may suggest that the bad boss is one who is guilty of extreme self-centeredness or suffers from a lack of compassion, we believe the reasons for most bad bossing are more often experiential rather than personal. For example, the bad boss might possess:
- a lack of experience or training;
- the absence of positive role models;
- limited awareness of the impact of their behavior;
- poor people-skills.

Many managers—both new and seasoned—make a simple, fundamental mistake: they think they need to tell people what to do. They feel as though they aren't an effective manager if they aren't bossing people around (after all, by definition the "boss" bosses, right?). That attitude is not surprising when we consider its genesis. The role models for many managers are their own bosses, primarily men and women who relied on the autocratic method to bully workers into doing what they wanted. What they typically don't realize is that based merely on title and rank, managers have tremendous power before they even utter a word or issue an order. Consequently, many managers don't understand the impact of this positional power and how to manage it for the best possible results.

At the other end of the spectrum are managers who let go totally of the reins or hand them over to their staff. Although they may come off as "good Joes," they, too, may be bad bosses. They don't, or can't, provide their people with a strong, clearly focused support system. Without a foundation upon which to build knowledge, experience and success, their employees are set up to flounder.

On another occasion Murray barged into Diane's office to ask her a question. While there Murray chastised Diane for being disorganized because she had piles of folders on her desk. Diane tried to explain to him that she was actually extremely organized; her folder system kept all of her ongoing projects within reach. She knew the contents of each and every folder—it was just that her style was different than his. She also reminded him that she consistently completed her projects and assignments on time and to his satisfaction. But Murray paid no attention to her comments. He demanded that she follow him down the hall to his office, where he flung open the door and pointed at his desk: not a single folder...not even a piece of paper. "This is what the desk of an organized manager looks like," he told Diane. "Now get back to your office and get organized."

Diane was understandably upset. Her boss didn't listen to her, and he clearly didn't accept her style of organization. He was demeaning and disrespectful. Two of her coworkers had witnessed the entire episode, adding immeasurably to her embarrassment and potentially undermining her authority as a team leader.

That night the entire regional executive team went out for a drink after work—without Murray. While the conversation began with Diane's experience that day, it rapidly evolved into a prolonged gripe session about Murray. Eventually Lee, a team member's husband, joined the group. He listened carefully to the discussion. Then, when there was a lull, he smiled at the team. "You know, I do consulting with many organizations, and I see this happening all the time. People work together all day then, after five, they get together to complain about the boss. If there's a lesson to be learned here, maybe it's this: no matter where you are on the ladder of success, there are people above and people below you. And when you look up, all you see is people's behinds."

Everyone laughed and the conversation moved away from Murray. Diane, however, could not stop picturing that ladder. She wondered if the people looking up at her were seeing what Lee had described. She knew that not all bosses were jerks, and she had no intention of becoming one! Diane was committed to finding a better way.

The Key Difference

What fundamentally separates the boss you remember as the best from the one you remember as the worst? When you pictured these two individuals, we would imagine that

you remembered some of their more prominent characteristics, but we also suspect you remember how they treated
their employees, and, more specifically, how they treated
you. Good bossing begins on the most basic level: kind-
ness, compassion and a profound sense of humanity.

The good bosses we tend to remember have good business skills and knowledge, and demonstrate the best aspects of human character. They impress us with their empathy instead of their authority. Rather than tossing out
challenges and watching who sinks or swims, they try to
make the difficult tasks as doable as possible.   They bring
big-picture perspective and clarity of direction to everyone
in the group; they help us stay motivated by acknowledging
our successes and helping us learn from and overcome our
mistakes; they make us feel like collaborators, not "person-
nel."   They inspire our trust. Their expectations are high,
and so are their values. They know that by respecting the
ideas and needs of each individual, they engender respect
and commitment. They provide ongoing individual feedback and *Performance Support* to enhance achievement of
goals. In this way, their people succeed while the bosses
garner support for their own leadership, and ultimately support for the vision and strategies of the entire organization.
In short, they make work a win-win-win proposition.

We believe the People*PACT* Principles and Process of
Humane Leadership define these core behaviors as well as
provide a critical tool for great bossing. Let us introduce
The People*PACT* principles and process here:

People*PACT*
Principles & Process of
Humane Leadership

People and their contributions are the core of any business. It is a leader's challenge and responsibility to support their people so they can do the best job possible. The following process and principles support producing exemplary performance and extraordinary results in business.

The *PACT* is a process that commits both the leader and the employee to mutually beneficial goals and support in accomplishing those goals. The *PACT* establishes strong alignment between what the organization needs from the employee as well as what the employee wants from their work experience. This level of understanding between boss and employee can significantly reduce conflict, misunderstanding and frustration, which in turn can further enhance productivity and performance. Creating and keeping the *PACT* through an ongoing process of *Performance Support* leads to exemplary achievement.

Perspective provides an opportunity for greater alignment and insight into the strategies and needs of the business. Understanding the big picture provides a context within which everyone can create a plan for personal success that also supports the goals of the organization. Understanding how their contribution fits in is critical. Having clarity of expectations and focus, and how this aligns with organizational goals, is key to great results.

Acknowledgement is the most inexpensive and simple way to create a positive, supporting and motivating environment. Specific, sincere acknowledgement is critical to encouraging growth, and is one of the most effective ways to positively impact the performance and behavior of people. It costs nothing. People grow through strength and confidence building, so a good leader encourages this at every reasonable opportunity.

Collaboration is the art of communicating and working effectively with others to spur innovation and results. Employees typically want to feel they are making a contribution, and are more motivated to achieve if they feel included as part of the larger effort. Participating, sharing ideas and learning new skills through collaboration and mutual support encourage a desire to "give back" through high performance.

Trust is the foundation for a thriving work environment. Transparency and humane truth-telling can be the ultimate trust builder. To create a trusting environment, where people feel safe enough to take risks is the best preparation for greatness. People feel free to be most creative and productive where there are no "failures", as long as learnings are gleaned from each experience. This is the kind of environment where high growth prevails and where people are happy, satisfied and give their best each day.

Where to Start

For Diane, as for most of us who want to be more effec-tive and compassionate managers, the process begins with a desire for a better way and the willingness to make per-sonal behavioral changes. Sometimes external changes can drive or influence the path of growth, as was the case with the next part of Diane's story.

Diane was becoming increasingly passionate about finding better ways to lead, even as the members of her executive team were looking for better places to work. Her co-workers were leaving in droves and the region's performance was going down the tubes. They were falling short in both quality of services and revenue. Diane believed the poor performance of the region re-lated directly to leadership problems. As the employee turnover rate continued to skyrocket, Diane's concerns about the future of the region grew.

Diane was seriously considering leaving, hoping to find a better boss who could be a mentor or, at least, an environment more conducive to growth and de-velopment. Her thoughts were interrupted when she was asked to attend an unscheduled executive staff meeting. The national CEO, Barbara, was there, and there was no sign of Murray. Barbara explained that the performance of the region was causing such great concern to the national office that they were bringing in a new regional president. She went on to assure the executive team that the organization would support Murray through this transition and do everything they could to find a good fit for him with another company.

To the surprise of many on the team, she also apologized that the national leadership had not dealt with this situation sooner. The change would begin with the arrival of a new president, Calvin, who was being transferred from the Northwest region.

Diane wondered about the future of the region and what would happen to her and her teammates if the situation deteriorated. Barbara's comments, however, did provide her with some hope: she had always heard great things about the Northwest Region and its leaders. Perhaps Calvin would turn out to be the mentor she so desperately wanted.

Diane was a loyal employee who was trying to make the best of the situation, but how long would she have stayed productive and positive while working for Murray? Diane was saved by the kind of leaders we are talking about. The CEO came in with a transparent, compassionate message. She even admitted fault and apologized. This display of humanity and willingness to effect positive change was the spark of hope this team needed. Let's see just how different respectful and competent leadership can be.

Leading to Success

The next Monday the new Regional President, Calvin, started his first day with an executive staff meeting. Instead of meeting in the main boardroom where Murray had always presided at the head of the ominous twenty-foot-long table, Calvin invited everyone into a small conference room around a circular table. Calvin met the executives at the door, greeting them one by one as they entered the room. He offered them each coffee or water, and he served it to them. Then he sat back, smiled, and began the meeting.

"To tell you the truth, I'm feeling a little nervous right now, imagining what may have been going through your minds over the weekend. I'd like to spend some time this morning talking about what you think are the key issues and priorities that need to be addressed. I'd like to begin by sharing some things about myself so I can become less of a stranger to you and learning a little about each of you as well. Is that okay with all of you?"

Everyone nodded.

Calvin continued, "So what are some of the things you'd like to know about me?"

Diane was so excited about the opportunity for open dialogue, she jumped right in.

"Could you describe your leadership style?" she asked him.

Calvin smiled and said, "I'm so happy to hear you asking about and using the term 'leadership.' I'd be happy to share my philosophies about it, and I invite you all to join in the dialogue as we go, so we can all get a feel for where we are at this point, as a team, on this crucial area."

Calvin had their undivided attention now. Murray's leadership philosophy, as he often shared, was about loyalty and performance coming from a strong commander. The executive team referred to it as Murray's "like-it-or-leave-it school of management."

*"I believe that people are the core of a business,"
Calvin told them. "And my most important role as your
leader is to support you in doing the best job that you
can so you can be successful—because when you're
successful, the company will be successful."*

*Diane glanced at her colleague, Matt. If the new pres-
ident was for real, he would be a breath of fresh air.*

*Calvin went on. "Certainly we also need a clear vi-
sion and strategy for the organization, and as a collective leadership team, I am confident we will develop
that quickly based on the experience you all bring to
the table. As your leader, I want to support you in your
individual professional development and support the
alignment of your personal goals with the goals of the
organization. I have more ideas, but I'd like to hear
from each of you first. What are your leadership philosophies?"*

*The dialogue flowed for two hours. Before Diane re-
turned to her office, she took Matt aside. "I think I may
have found my mentor," she told him.*

It is amazing the difference a good boss—and a good
leader—can make.

Where You Can Go From Here

As you will see, Calvin was beginning to set the stage
for creating The *PACT*. He was being transparent, bringing the bigger picture perspective, acknowledging people
and asking questions to learn more about each member
of his team. He was talking about aligning the organizational goals with their individual goals and he talked about

learning how he could support them in achieving their personal professional goals.

This book will describe this process in detail, so that you can use it to become a better boss through supporting greater performance. This approach includes a greater focus on leadership and treating employees with respect, dignity, fairness, and honor. It means reducing fear and maximizing trust in the workplace. It also means setting clear roles, responsibilities and expectations while providing the tools and ongoing support needed to accomplish them. Compassionate leaders understand that mistakes happen and react in a reasonable, responsible, and compassionate way when they do. Most of all, great bossing is promoting people's success and not dwelling on their failure. It's about treating people like they "can," then helping to make sure that they "do." The strategies you will find in this book have been shown to make businesses grow by helping the people who work there grow. They will also improve the quality of life for everyone, including bosses, employees (and their family members) and customers.

There are some simple, straightforward benefits that people typically want in the workplace:

- They want to experience fairness and respect;
- They want to feel that the company is just as committed to their success as they are expected to be to the company's;
- They want to feel like they are making a contribution;
- They want to know there is support for their development;
- They want to know that what they do each day will eventually lead to something better;

- AND, they want a boss who understands and supports the concept that most people learn, grow and lead productive lives both in and out of the office. They want a boss who realizes that each employee brings to work a uniquely personal set of desires, talents and goals that cross over from their private to their professional lives.

Why Make The *PACT*?

Making the *PACT* with each of your employees could be the single most effective action you ever take towards becoming an effective leader. To make the *PACT*, the leader engages employees in an ongoing dialogue about roles, responsibilities and expectations. Additionally, a good boss asks each employee to specify what they want from the company and their careers. Then, the good boss commits to supporting employees on their path to attaining their goals. He/she customizes his approach to meet each person's specific needs in a reasonable and appropriate way. Bosses are sometimes surprised by the responses they hear when they ask about individuals' goals:

- Some people want more time with their families or more vacation time each year;
- Some need higher pay or expanded benefits;
- Some want to learn new skills and abilities or find greater challenges on the job, while others have a skill or ability that is not being used that they would like to incorporate;
- And some, of course, want to get promoted or be the boss. (Interestingly, far fewer than you would expect actually want to be the boss!)

Whatever goals or motivators the employee values strongly, the point is this: when you enact a *PACT* with an employee in a safe environment where trust is present, you may not only be surprised by what it is they actually want, but also how easy it might be to help deliver. We have seen again and again that employees who feel valued and whose needs are seriously considered work harder and more effectively than others.

What's in it for You?

Now that you are a leader, it is easy to see how, without employee commitment and loyalty, your team will not produce the innovative new ideas you need to be competitive. Nor will you see the performance you need from your employees to sustain and grow your business. People need leaders who believe in and practice a balanced lifestyle. People need courtesy and caring in the workplace today, particularly since they often spend so much time in their offices. Managers and employees need the kind of people skills that will support a safe and trusting environment. Employees want to work more independently and have the freedom to be more creative while still being a member of a high functioning team. Managers need to use bossing techniques that support and encourage this independence and creativity as well as capitalize on the value of team performance.

We believe that the practice of compassionate leadership must be woven into the core of the fabric of everyday life in the workplace so everyone—employer, employee and manager—can prosper. We believe the world needs more of this kind of new leadership that is inclusive and collaborative rather than combative and divisive.

How much more successful could your team and your organization be with more people-centered, *performance supporting* bossing? The People*PACT* will transform your employee management experience from frustrating, inconsistent and haphazard to systematic, energetic and successful.

We challenge you to seek more compassionate ways to lead, and to provide more consistent, humane *Performance Support.* We then expect that you will find what we have discovered: this approach yields outstanding results through exemplary performance.

Chapter 2
THE PEOPLE*PACT* PROCESS

"We tend to get what we expect."

— *John F. Kennedy*

How to Create the *PACT*

The way people do a job is a professional fingerprint, an indelible stamp impressing their style on every project, product and problem that crosses their desks. When a manager focuses only on the job at hand, ignoring the distinctive needs and desires of his team members, difficulties arise.

It is important to focus on the individual differences that your team members bring to the workplace and the systematic development of individual talent and strengths rather than on weakness and "improvement." But how do you enact the *PACT* in a way that can also benefit the whole team? And how do you lead from a people-first perspective while maintaining your balance with operations, your boss and your other responsibilities? Making the *PACT* will propel you to achieve these goals.

Customize Your Approach
for Win-Win Results

Although bosses often hear employees expressing similar professional goals—growth, recognition and advancement, for example—we have found in our experience that individual employees actually differ greatly on the issue of professional and personal goals. Often they respond to these questions with what they believe the manager wants to hear; they only reveal their real goals in a safe, supportive environment which encourages truth-telling and individual growth.

Since each person that you work with is a unique human being with his or her own needs and dreams, the compassionate boss has the opportunity, as well as the responsibility, to reasonably support these needs and dreams. In so doing, the employee/boss relationship can shift from one of intimidation and manipulation to affirmation and collaboration. While this may take more skill, time and effort for the boss up front, in the long run happy employees produce more and create far fewer problems and headaches for their managers. Obviously, the payoff can be tremendous—in time utilization, quality of life and the bottom-line.

Process Means Consistency

The *PACT* is the agreement between you and your employee. It concerns the authentic, ambitious and personal goals each of you has. It includes much more than the typical formal process your company uses to set and track goals and objectives. The *PACT* does not eliminate the formal evaluation process; it supplements it. You will be amazed at how easily the formal process proceeds within the context of the *PACT*.

Let's take a look at how Calvin set the *PACT* within 30 days of his arrival.

During his first week on the job, Calvin set up individual meetings with each of his direct reports. His first meeting was with John, VP of Sales. He began by reiterating his leadership philosophy, stressing that one of his key responsibilities was to support his team. In that spirit of support, he asked John what he felt was important about his job. Calvin quickly learned that John was not interested in further climbing of the corporate ladder, rather, he truly wanted to be the company "guru" of the sales process...he wanted to be the "master" of sales. John wanted to support the development of a sales training process that would be the best in the country. He wanted to mentor sales associates; he felt his years of experience in the field would serve him well in this role, and that he would significantly benefit the company through training exemplary sales persons.

John couldn't imagine a more satisfying way to spend the last ten years of his career. Calvin made a commitment to John to support his goals, seeing the value in this proposal to both John and the organization. The company was developing a national corporate university, and he promised to advocate for John to lead the sales division efforts. Additionally, Calvin and John agreed that some of the basic skills important to sales were also critical to customer service. Calvin asked John if he would be interested in collaborating with the Customer Service training area to incorporate those skill sets into their training modules. Finally, Calvin made a commitment to John to continue to look for opportunities where John's skills, knowledge and passion for teaching could be leveraged to serve the organization. They agreed that they would review these opportunities at their routine monthly individual meetings. John went home that night and shared with his wife that he had not been so excited about his job and his future with the organization since the day he was hired!

To further witness how the *PACT*'ing process goes, let's see how Calvin worked with Diane and another member of his team.

Diane's view of her future was very different from John's. Being the newest and youngest member of the team, Diane had over 25 years to look forward to in her career. She intended to continue moving to higher levels of leadership. She had a lot to learn about the organization and was very interested in aspects of the company beyond her current area of marketing. She hoped one day to rise to the level of Regional President and knew she needed to both learn the business and enhance her leadership skills.

Calvin had already come to appreciate Diane's talents and agreed that she had significant potential. Calvin made the commitment to Diane to continue to look for opportunities where she could participate on interdisciplinary project teams, allowing her to learn more about other areas of the business. In doing so, Diane could gain a broader perspective of the organization and an awareness of how each area fit into the overall corporate picture. Additionally, he would look for leadership skill-building opportunities for her, including leading teams and participating in specific training efforts. Calvin promised Diane that this would be part of their ongoing conversation about her growth and development.

In his third meeting that day, Calvin was truly taken by the candor exhibited by David, his VP of Finance. David told Calvin that his wife had died from breast cancer six months earlier and how difficult that experience had been for him and his children. He admitted that although he probably had not given 100% to work in those past six months, he had found some solace in work and felt that he had made some significant gains in the department. Calvin acknowledged David for doing such a great job with the department, particularly under such difficult circumstances. Calvin knew of several of David's initiatives that had become models for all the other regions. When Calvin asked David what was most important to him professionally, David responded that while he was committed to continuing a high level of performance, a flexible work schedule and reduced travel was most important, so he could be more available to his children.

David certainly did not want special treatment, but he wanted the flexibility to leave work for an hour to attend a morning program at the elementary school where his daughter was singing in a recital, for example. Certainly he did not want this kind of flexible schedule to burden his team or his colleagues and

promised that the time away would in no way nega-
tively impact his productivity or leadership of his team.
Calvin was aware of David's track record and capabili-
ties. He told David he would support such flexibility as
much as he could. Additionally, until David told him
he was ready to take on special projects, Calvin would
help deflect those requests so that no additional re-
sponsibilities would be thrown on David's plate. Calvin
made it clear to David that by not taking on any special
projects, David would not be eligible for the Special
Projects Bonus. David agreed that the opportunity to
support his children was much more important to him
than any bonus right now.

The suggestion that you move, as a leader, from a single, simple standard evenly applied to everyone to a people-first, individualized approach can appear to be a messy, even chaotic prospect. In fact, nothing could be further from the truth. The *PACT* is a method that is all about discovering the differences in people and working towards turning them into a winning advantage. It is a standard process that spotlights each individual employee's unique goals and aspirations, and then uses those personal motivators as fuel to move the entire team forward. It is a strategy that couples individual perspectives with a consistent process that includes clearly defining roles, responsibilities and expectations. It is a plan that charts a course for employee growth, satisfaction and accomplishment which, in turn, leads to unparalleled organizational success.

As you can see from the three examples above, one of the key ingredients to a successful *PACT*'ing process is honesty and trust on both sides. Each of these three employees felt comfortable enough to be candid with Calvin, as they believed in his intention and sincerity to support them. John didn't feel he had to express the desire to "climb the corporate ladder;" Diane felt safe enough with Calvin to share her dreams of significant career growth, even at such an early stage of her journey; and David showed courage and trust in Calvin by being very honest about his personal situation. Through his openness at their initial meeting, Calvin had already begun to establish a trusting relationship with these team members which could enable such honesty. To continue this core *PACT*-setting dialogue, Calvin held ongoing bi-weekly "update conversations" with each of these employees which helped to further establish the relationship. During these meetings, Calvin got to know each of the individuals professionally and personally. Sharing information about himself helped create a safe environment. He also followed through on his commitments of support. This all helps to build trust, authenticity and honesty.

The *PACT* does not need a formal document (although it can be), but it does symbolize your pledge. You make a *PACT* with your employees that you will treat them with complete humaneness, with respect and commitment to support their individual needs in balance with the organization's needs. You pledge to do specific things that can help them reach their personal goals in exchange for their commitment to fulfill the goals you set for the team and those required by the organization. Simply put, the *PACT* strikes a balance between what each employee wants as a measure of personal success and what the company needs to be a success.

In truth, the People*PACT* process begins the instant you, as boss, depart from the "conformity" model of the past and

turn toward a "diversity model" where different styles and
methods of performance are valued. On a nuts and bolts
level, however, the *PACT* begins with a conversation and
continues as an ongoing series of conversations which are
all part of the *Performance Support* process. Consider this
example:

*Diane is now anxious to support her direct reports'
individual professional goals and dreams.   She had
been in the department for about two years when the
company made her a manager of a newly created marketing unit. In forming the unit, they pulled in people
from several other areas including the one in which
Diane worked. Many of the new members of her team
were former peers. Not only had they socialized, but
they also knew stories about each other going back
many years.*

*One day, Diane was having a meeting with Chuck,
a former co-worker who was now a direct report, to
discuss what he wanted to accomplish over the next
few years with his assigned group of customers. His
answer was blunt: "I don't want to do anything beyond
what I have to do. I will be conscientious and thorough but really, Diane, I just want to be left alone."*

*Diane was stunned. Obviously, this was a diffi-
cult conversation for both of them. Chuck was visibly
distressed, sweating and shaking. Diane was feeling
some heat herself. Calvin had told her that he wanted
everyone to begin working with the new programs the
company had designed. She needed Chuck on her
side! But when she probed, Chuck seemed adamant.
"You may want to be all bright-eyed and bushy-tailed*

for the higher ups, but don't count me in on that!" he told her.

Diane knew that Chuck could produce. She sincerely wanted to support Chuck and let him work the way he felt he worked best, so she asked him, "Chuck, I really want this to work well for both of us, so please help me to understand what you said. Would you please describe what 'leave me alone' would look like to you?"

Chuck was quick to answer. "Well, unless there is some emergency, I would appreciate our just reviewing the monthly reports, so we both agree on how I'm doing. In the meantime, since I've been doing this job for 16 years, I'd appreciate you just letting me do what I do best. If we see problems with the reports, then we'll cross that bridge when we come to it."

Diane had set up her department to submit feedback weekly, and Chuck's request ran contrary to this method. Nevertheless, she considered his suggestion. Diane knew that Chuck had had a difficult time with a previous micro-managing boss who had nearly caused him to be fired. She wondered if that experience was behind his lack of willingness to cooperate. "Okay, Chuck," she said, "I know you're a good worker and that your customers like you. If you continue to meet the required company goals, then I'll do my best to leave you alone except for monthly reports."

Over the next several months, Diane and Chuck kept their bargain with each other. One day, during a report review, after Diane had congratulated him on a great month, Chuck gave her a positive message in return. "You've been very fair with me, Diane," he said.

"I know I gave you a hard time at first, but I just didn't feel like I had the energy to get all 'corporate' at this stage of my career. I really appreciate that you were willing to be flexible with me."

Over time, Diane and Chuck developed a deep trust. One day during a review, Chuck confided to Diane that if he could get a promotion to Senior Associate, he would be able to retire happy. The promotion would let everyone know that he had been a valuable employee, despite what his previous boss had believed.

Diane told him she thought she could help, but they would have to make a new agreement about how they worked together and clarify their expectations. Among other things, he would need to work on some special projects, those that he had avoided before, and she would need enhanced communication; they would develop a plan that, in return should result in a promotion for him within two years.

Twenty months later, Chuck was rewarded. The two of them marveled together on what he had been willing to do to achieve his goal. "Who could have foreseen that I would be willing to develop one of those new computer programs?" Chuck laughed. "And no one could have told me I would have actually gotten an award for doing the new company customer programs, either! Thanks, Diane! You've been great."

The agreement, or *PACT*, between Diane and Chuck evolved significantly over time. This is part of the process. Your ongoing meetings with employees help keep both of you up to date with how things progress, change or are road-blocked, which allows you the opportunity to appropriately adjust your agreements in a timely manner. Diane and Chuck's *PACT* was a huge success. Of course, it would not have worked if both had not carefully kept their word. Over time and in pressure situations, it can be difficult for a manager to keep her promises, especially when business conditions or policies change. Nevertheless, the *PACT* is a promise, and it is crucial that you keep your word. Even one broken agreement can undermine your credibility with the entire team. If circumstances change, both parties can agree to redefine the *PACT*. Employees will appreciate the candor and commitment you demonstrate by admitting your vulnerability to organizational upheaval and promptly renegotiating your agreement with them.

Start at the Very Beginning!

In an ideal world, the best time to begin making a *PACT* with an employee is the day he or she is hired. Clarifying expectations—yours, the employee's and the organization's—puts everybody on the same page. It also minimizes the potential for misunderstanding and disappointment on all sides. Just bear in mind that the *PACT* is a process—specifically, a process with trust at its core. Since trust has only begun to be established at the time of hire, a final *PACT* may not be possible at that point, however, the first day on the job is a great time to set the stage and begin the conversations.

There are multiple players to consider when developing the *PACT*: the employee, you and your team, and the organization. And there is no better opportunity than the time of hire to make those positions known. Most bosses are pretty clear when it comes to explaining to an interviewee what is expected of them. They do a pretty good job of reviewing the demands of the position, key goals and objectives. *PACT* bosses will also discuss the team's and organization's needs and goals. What are the needs of the team as well as the overall organizational expectations of this employee? Whether the organization is rebuilding, booming, expanding, changing its focus or reorganizing after cutbacks, it is important that the employee feels a part of the larger effort.   Once you have provided your employee with this bigger picture perspective, you can begin to discuss his or her professional goals.

Exploring an Employee's Needs and Aspirations

The openness of *PACT*'ing can be disconcerting to workers who have spent a lifetime—or what seemed like one—in authoritarian offices. Faced with the possibility of giving the "wrong" answer to a traditional manager, many new hires will simply tell you what they believe you want to hear. We suggest that you put aside broad, generic questions and focus specifically on queries that reveal the employee's unique perspective. Questions like, "Tell me a little about what's really important to you in a job?" or "What contribution to your last job are you most proud of?" reveals something about an employee's preferences, strengths or work style.   They also set up the kind of meaningful dialogue that builds trust. Keep it going! Ask some important follow-up questions.   Since past behavior can be a predictor of future performance, focus on pivotal periods of the person's life. Questions like, "What made you choose Yale instead of Harvard?" or "Why marketing over a degree in finance?" will get you meaty answers, the kinds that offer you a glimpse into a new hire's inner workings. They will also enable you to build a profile so you can begin to work to each employee's talents and preferences. Over time, as trust deepens, you can learn even more by asking "What difficulties did you encounter in your last job and what did you learn from them?"

Don't forget to share similar experiences about your own background. Although the *PACT* conversations should remain principally focused on the employee, sharing a little about yourself helps to build the relationship and trust. This is particularly helpful when you share some of your past difficulties and what you learned from them. Such stories can humanize you, allowing you to be more authentic with your employee. Keep in mind however, this is not about "true confessions" or sharing stories that you would not feel comfortable sharing with many others.

Finally, invite your new employee into the *PACT*. Tell him that one of your most important roles as boss is to help your employees excel in their positions. Ask your employee to allow time to get to know the job and organization a bit better. Suggest that, with some acclimation to the position and company, the employee consider how the demands of the job line up with personal goals. Then continue the informal conversations with periodic updates. Finally, set a date to discuss specifically how you can help optimize this particular professional experience. What does the employee want? What can you do to provide better support? Make the *PACT*! You can even follow up this conversation with an email confirming your commitment to support the employee. In some organizations, there is space on the performance plan document that allows for such comments.

For most employees, there is a tremendous amount of information to gather and sort between the time of hire and the date of the first evaluation. For a new employee in a *PACT* team, there additional new things to absorb! Your unique perspective, the team's openness and the collaborative environment you have built may be an eye-opening experience for a new worker. And, once they have had time to observe how their colleagues handle autonomy and the high level of trust present in the environment, they will certainly want to participate.

By now, it has been several months since the employee started on the new job. It is time to have the in-depth *PACT* discussion. Establishing and maintaining trust takes great courage for both boss and worker. You, as boss, must trust that employees have the organization's best interests at heart, and that these interests are balanced with their own. Employees need to be reassured that what they say will not come back to haunt them. Put them at ease by reaffirming that you are on their side. You might say something like, "You've done very well in your first three months here. You've fulfilled both the team and the organization's needs. And now, what about your want? Is the job working out for you? What can we do to make your situation better?" Together, you can then explore any scenarios employees believe will enhance their performance, including growth and development issues, the possibility of educational benefits, a more rewarding work/home interface or whatever else might boost morale and participation.

What a *PACT* boss needs to do, in a non-threatening way, is to take a proactive stance. Stay in close contact with every new employee so that the situation can't go awry. This could be anywhere from weekly to daily with a new employee. Then, if the employee hits a bump in the road, ask her what she feels she needs to pull her performance up. The idea is to set your people up to win. Avoid the constant search for deficiencies and problems, although you certainly should address them as they come up, but rather look for ways to help. It is in the *PACT* boss's best interest to support employees' plans and projects and work to ensure that they won't fail. For those situations that require daily check-ins ensure they are done in a spirit of collaboration; remember, your role is as a partner in your team members' success—not as a micro-manager or inspector. The continued and growing success of each of your people is your goal. In that context, support flows naturally and the employee blooms.

Not Just for New Employees

It is important to make the *PACT* and keep it updated with all employees, not just new hires. You may be in a situation where you are the new boss, such as Calvin was, or you may not have done this before and want to start it now with your tenured team. Whatever the case, you can follow the same steps outlined in this book, regardless of the tenure of the employee. Your timing might be somewhat different with someone who has been in the job a while, as they may have a better understanding of what they want from it compared to the new employee. Your seasoned employee might be ready to jump in right away, however, we still encourage you to go through the steps and ask those key questions (see *Steps to Making the PACT*, Appendix A), as it helps the employee better understand the process and the benefits of the *PACT*.

Steadfast *PACT*'ing in Changing Times

These days you only need to pick up the newspaper to become aware of what a difference a day makes, particularly in the business world. Economic fluctuations, leadership crises and even slight day-to-day adjustments can change the big picture, even as you're painting it for your employees. Such upheavals, minor and major, can pose a challenge to the *PACT* boss. They also make the *PACT* objectives—*perspective, acknowledgement, collaboration and trust*—more crucial to you and your team members.

If your employees, the organization you work for and yes, you yourself, were not constantly evolving, there would be little impetus for a long and satisfying career! In the next chapter, you will discover how the creative, resilient *PACT* boss supports the *PACT* and his or her people in the face of the only certainty: change!

Chapter 3
SUPPORTING THE *PACT*

"We can't solve problems by using the same kind of think-ing we used when we created them."

— *Albert Einstein*

Keeping the *PACT* and Working Through Some of the Challenges

The *PACT*, as you have enacted it, is a snapshot of a par-ticular moment in time. It reflects your goals and hopes and needs—and those of your employees—at a specific time and stage in your careers. In reality, though, a healthy *PACT* is vital and organic, a dynamic and evolving work-in-progress. At any given moment, an employee's needs, or yours as boss, or the company's, may take a sudden detour from the path that seemed so right just yesterday. In cases like these, staying the course is not only unwise, but it can also seem irresponsible, indifferent or unresponsive to the people around you. This chapter is about ongoing *PACT* maintenance and adjustment. It shows you how to ensure you have a *PACT* that is strong enough to support you, your team and your company, yet flexible enough to grow in accordance with changing circumstances. It will also show you how to work through some of the common challenges and sidestep the common pitfalls that can shake even the strongest agreement.

Creating the Foolproof *PACT* Through *Performance Support*

"Give them an inch, they'll take a mile." We've all heard that saying. Some of us have even managed in accordance with it. But with what success? People do their best work, become more accountable and perform above and beyond expectations when they feel they are investing their efforts in a boss who has also invested in them. But can employees take advantage of a *PACT* situation? Not if you set it up clearly, frequently follow up to discuss how both of you are holding up your ends of the *PACT*, and make fair and reasonable adjustments if situations change.

We'd like to begin here by defining a new term: *Performance Support*. While management may be about direction and organization, true leadership is about supporting performance. Today's managers and leaders must do both, providing those around you with the tools, resources, training and ongoing clarity, mentorship, support and guidance needed to do the best job they possibly can. This sets up a best-success scenario for the organization, the individual, and the longevity of the *PACT*. This process is so critical, we have dedicated the majority of Chapter 6 to it. It is through the *Performance Support* Process that you both create and sustain the *PACT*.

PACT Challenges:
Unrealistic Requests

In work and life, it's often the simple things that count the most. That's why nearly all employees are happy to provide their bosses with clear *PACT* requests. An early afternoon off once a month to transport an elderly parent to a doctor's appointment may be all it takes to ease the stress for a worker torn between caring for a loved one and attending to his job. For someone else, a key role on a certain committee can breathe new life into a very familiar, even mundane position.

Occasionally, however, an employee's requests extend beyond the reasonable realm of typical—even beyond the manager's ability to accept them without some degree of risk. Such was the case with Alan, a talented new customer service representative who reported to Linda, Diane's colleague on the senior management team.

Alan was a recently-graduated Physician's Assistant, who decided that he wanted to take his scientific knowledge into administration. Alan was a personable guy whose winning ways had made him a success. Linda recognized his knowledge and talent and hired him on the spot.

At the time of Alan's first evaluation he was thriving in the corporate atmosphere. He made a seamless transition into the environment and met every challenge presented to him. Alan's new boss Linda had brainstormed with Diane in advance of this meeting with Alan. Linda admired how Diane had embraced Calvin's PACT approach and wanted her input on do-

ing the same with Alan. Linda was interested to hear how such a well-rounded, gregarious, talented man might respond when asked what would make his job more satisfying for him. When he did give his answer, it was even more remarkable than she could have imagined.

"I want to be CEO of this organization in five years. I want to run this company," Alan announced with a smile. "But for right now what I want is the highest possible annual review rating given."

Certainly, Alan's request seemed unrealistic. Although his background included a great education, he had few skills to qualify him for his dream job, and five years was hardly enough time to develop those skills. Still, if what energized and motivated Alan was the prospect of being "on top," wasn't it worth exploring the ways he could work toward achieving his dream?

After Linda and Alan laughed together at his unbridled ambition, they considered the realities of Alan's situation. Though Linda could not make any promises about Alan's "five-year plan," there were certainly an abundance of career opportunities at their company. She would offer him every chance to develop his leadership skills. As far as Alan earning the highest possible rating, however, the situation was a bit more iffy. First year employees were simply not given the highest rating on evaluations.

But Alan was unwilling to let the issue go. What would any employee—new or veteran—have to do to earn such a rating? He would go that distance and beyond. After a great deal of discussion, Linda drew her line in the sand. In order to qualify, he would have to go significantly above and beyond the baseline expectations of the job. Alan would have to design and execute four Special Projects—projects so astounding that the reports would impress not only Linda, but also Calvin, Calvin's boss, and his senior team. In addition, Alan would have to achieve the best call ratings of anyone on the team and so amaze the customers that they actually called the company to sing his praises. The list, Linda admits, was daunting. Yet, it was what Diane believed would launch Alan down the road he had imagined for himself. He was a tireless, committed worker, and at the end of his first year he had fulfilled all of Linda's conditions.

Were Linda's demands extreme? Yes they were, but what Alan wanted was also extreme, and he was willing to pay the price. He got his high evaluation, and he truly earned it. Although he is not CEO at that company (yet!), he is in a very high ranking position and still going strong. Linda's decision to consider stretching accepted policy turned out to be a win-win-win situation for Alan, her, and the organization.

So what can we learn about supporting the *PACT* from this scenario? When an employee's request seems unrealistic or even outrageous, it's important not to overreact. ("You want *my* job? I don't think so!") Instead, ask questions that will draw out the reason she set this specific goal. If a particular position appeals to her because she enjoys autonomy, build more opportunities for independence into her position. If a human resources employee feels she has a knack for PR, allow her to get her feet wet by writing the department's press releases. Provide the worker reaching for the higher rungs of the ladder with smaller steps to her goal and you allow the person to discover herself without endangering her career or team stability. You also offer her the opportunity to develop a more practical view of her goals, the challenges along the career path she has chosen and how long it might take to reach the level she considers her destination.

Challenge: *Employee with extraordinarily high (seemingly unrealistic) goals.*

Solution: *Don't overreact. Ask questions to better understand the reasons behind their goals. Discuss core skills and experiences it takes to achieve that goal. Find ways to help them build those skills/experiences, step by step.*

Remember: the People*PACT* is based upon support and respect. Some employees, like Alan, are willing and able to pay a high price to attain a goal. If, on the other hand, a team member's *PACT* goals are too big to juggle along with her other goals—her personal life, her family, or an unstated agenda—a manageable, step-by-step plan enables her to reassess and, if necessary, scale back. Whatever the result, your employees will feel supported by a boss who understands what is important to them, and that is the essence of People*PACT* thinking.

A Question of Fairness

Mary was the single mother of twin sons. While her boys were in elementary school, Mary's family and professional duties were relatively easy to work out. She dropped the boys off at school on her way to work then picked them up from an after-school program on her way home. When the boys entered middle school, however, managing the situation was no longer so simple.

The before and after-school programs seemed to evaporate when the boys reached middle school. And while one of her sons, Jake, was able to stay home alone and behave responsibly, his brother, Jason, was not so mature. It took Mary weeks to patch together a workable schedule for the boys, and even after she did, she still came up short. She needed to leave work early one day a week to drive Jason to and from the tutoring program Mary hoped would keep him from failing math.

Mary was a good, reliable worker, the kind of employee who was at her desk early nearly every day. Her boss, Diane, was happy to offer her the few hours she needed in exchange for coming in early three days a week. But when Mary began missing Wednesday afternoon meetings, she aroused her coworkers' irritation. When they began having to schedule conference calls and discussions around her schedule, the resentment began to build.

This scenario is every boss's nightmare: accommodating special needs of employees, only to raise the ire of those who feel the treatment is unfair. Mary's story illustrates a humane and individualized approach on behalf of the boss but not a complete *PACT*. Mary's "payment" for her special treatment wasn't clear to others. Diane did not make accommodations to cover her responsibilities during that time. A few more crucial steps could have turned this into a winning scenario and model *PACT* arrangement.

Special arrangements like those provided to Mary require explanation to the team to avoid the appearance of favoritism. Diane did take this issue to the next team meeting with the following discussion points:

- Clarified issue: Mary's need to spend an afternoon every week away from her desk to support her family. (Note: Mary agreed this was OK to share with team);
- Clarify "fairness" of core accommodation: what, specifically, Mary will do to make up the time;
- Brain-storm possible consequences/inconveniences to team members due to this accommodation for Mary;
- Brain-storm solutions and adaptations needed to make to ensure that all team members, including Mary, could meet their goals.

Since the *PACT* is a win-win-win proposition, any agreement is best when it benefits the employee, the boss and the organization. Where *PACT*'ing is the order of the day, these deals are easily made and maintained. That's because when each employee enacts a *PACT* and everyone is getting what they need to succeed, there is little opportunity to complain of "favoritism." While a single parent like Mary may need some flexibility with time, a development-minded worker may need exposure to certain projects or participation on committees. If both have their way and the team is working smoothly, all sides are satisfied.

> **Pitfall:** *Making a commitment with one employee that can have possible negative or inconvenient consequences on other employees.*
>
> **Solution:** *Transparency: discuss the situation with team before completing the PACT; they may have even better solutions. Regardless, when they are asked to participate in finding the solution, they are more apt to support it.*

Of course, life can be complicated. You may encounter a valuable employee whose needs seem to extend beyond the limits of fairness or even run counter to company policy. While clearly no *PACT* should venture into truly inappropriate territory (e.g., illegal, immoral, or unethical actions), we have found that if an employee is willing to fulfill his end of the bargain to get what he feels he needs, almost anything can be achieved. For example, we have worked in companies with very firm vacation policies yet have managed to *PACT* with employees who had planned and paid for trips that extended beyond the time off they had earned. Employees have exchanged an additional week of vacation for on-the-job effort of equal value: perhaps several weeks of very-focused overtime devoted to the completion of a specific project or presentation that will reduce the burden on the rest of the team. Remember: creativity within reason is the winning formula.

Whatever the bargaining chips available to you as boss, it is good to remember that time-off is one of the aces you hold as manager. Whether you are bargaining hard for a new employee or making a *PACT* with a valued company veteran, some flexibility in the rest and relaxation department can reap you big benefits as manager and for the team as a whole. Just bear in mind that fairness, like a beautifully enacted *PACT*, is important. Anyone who sees part of the deal needs to have some idea of the other side and see it as equitable. Our feeling is that if you feel you can pass the "red-face test," that is, if you were to share the details of the arrangement you've made with your CEO or Board Chairman and feel good about it, then you've done the right thing. It is important to point out, of course, that any accommodations have to fall within what is legal and acceptable as dictated by company policy.

Workplaces, like families, are at their most fair when employees are valued equitably and individually; that is, with some consideration of the unique characteristics, talents and yes, needs, each member brings to the table. How can you as a boss build morale and mutual trust while keeping dissent from the ranks at a minimum? Transparency is key here. Open communication with the team and in some cases, engaging them in solution-building can avoid potential resentment. And, of course, when each individual has their own *PACT*, and knows the boss is also supporting them in a "special" way, they are typically much more supportive to making accommodations for their colleagues.

A Strategy for Success

No matter how tight the team, the people in your group will always offer a unique compilation of undiscovered strengths, undisclosed dreams and untapped talents. Additionally, you can plan on a range of talent and performance across any team or work group. It is important to keep a realistic perspective on this support process, a perspective that actually applies to all aspects of bossing: don't expect to achieve 100% effectiveness. Typically, there is a small percentage of employees, many estimate 10% or so, who don't respond, cooperate or perform at an acceptable level. They are often resistant to change, loose canons, saboteurs, or just unresponsive to coaching for improvement; we call them the "Resisters." This is a reality of bossing and an important expectation for you to keep in mind. Nevertheless, you cannot allow your hopes for the team and the organization to be governed by a small minority. A few nay-sayers shouldn't prevent you from doing everything you can to support your people. Although we suggest to not give-up on the Resisters, we highly recommend that you don't over focus your time and efforts on them either. Simply reap the benefits of the success you will enjoy with the majority of your group and take comfort in the knowledge that you have made a solid and sincere effort with the Resisters, too. Ultimately, they may succumb to the temptation to be their best rather than to remain cynical, pessimistic or stagnant, or, they might move on.

> **Challenge:** *Nay-sayers or Resisters who complain or criticize the PACT process*
>
> **Solution:** *Be transparent; be fair and equitable; remind them of their own personal PACT and how you are supporting them; don't focus an inordinate amount of time on the squeaky wheel compared to other team members.*

By enacting the *PACT*, you set in motion a process that is all about discovering the differences in people and working to turn them into valuable assets to your team. By treating the men and women who work for you as unique individuals, you transform their individual goals and aspirations into the fuel that moves the entire team forward.

Remember, The People*PACT* is a process, and process means consistency over time. It can be difficult for a manager to keep these agreements with employees. Nevertheless, it is crucial that you continue to build on the trust you have established through acknowledgement, collaboration and support. The *PACT* principles have made it possible to create and maintain an environment that isn't driven by fear and intimidation, and steadfastly supports the goals of the organization. It is OK if you try something and it doesn't work out. Discuss the situation openly with your team, modeling how you handle their failed experiments by finding the learnings in it. It is often those difficult situations that offer the most opportunity to build relationships, hone leadership skills and create a climate where support, responsibility and honesty are often the most valuable currency. Commitment and persistence to maintaining the *PACT* process reaps tremendous rewards and achievements for all.

Chapter 4
PEOPLE MAKE THE DIFFERENCE

"If everyone is thinking alike then somebody isn't thinking."
— *George S. Patton*

Supporting People in Great Performance

The Value of Interpersonal Skills in Making & Keeping the *PACT*

Creating a collegial, productive, supportive workplace is one of the most challenging tasks a leader faces. Indeed, this may be the most critical responsibility of any leader. Not only must the leader set a stellar example in this arena by having healthy, effective, positive working relationships with colleagues, direct reports and supervisors, but they must also support others in becoming similarly adept in this more human realm of workplace interactions.

Derailed on the Road to Success

How often have you seen great plans and systems get sidetracked—or even destroyed—because they were road-blocked by emotions, egos, inability to compromise, or personal agendas? This list of "humanness" can go on and on, as it often does in our daily work lives. Take Jake for example, who was leading the innovation team in Diane's department last year. His team's story illustrates what happens when hidden agendas and fear get in the way of effective performance.

Jake had two trainers, two marketing & sales managers, a physician, a nurse and a strategic planner on the team he was leading. They were challenged with the task of developing new employer health education services. Initially everyone was very excited about the opportunity to participate in this project. The team set formal goals for itself and defined roles for each member. Things were rolling along during the first month, with a creative stream of ideas for products flowing from all the team members.

Then, when it was time to begin prioritizing potential education modules for further research and development, a shift began to occur within the team. Here is an example of what was transpiring:

One day Jake was leading a team discussion with the goal of taking the twenty modules that had been originally proposed and researched and shaving the list down to ten. A heated argument erupted. Mitch, the sales manager, became very resistant to Jake's suggestion to eliminate one of the modules Mitch had originally proposed. Mitch argued that his module would prove to be the most beneficial to the program in the long run, even though the team's opportunity research had shown that market data did not support his belief. Mitch felt so strongly about his position that he stormed out of the meeting and called in sick the next day. Jake was so shaken by the outburst, that he adjourned the meeting, suggesting everyone rethink the priorities.

In the meantime, Mitch began sending emails and voicemails to others in the organization questioning the validity of the Innovation Team's process. This was extremely upsetting to Jake and the rest of the team. Jake then had to spend a significant amount of time explaining Mitch's complaints and defending the project. This was an unfortunate waste of time and energy, especially considering this project and team had been originally developed and sanctioned by senior leadership. Jake became so paralyzed by the potential conflict and ultimate possibility of failure of his team's effort that he transferred to a different position. He did not tell Diane the real reason for leaving; rather he stated that the new position was a great career opportunity for him. Diane had to scramble to find new leadership for the team, along with dealing with Mitch and the havoc he raised.

In hind sight, Diane realized that she made a number of mistakes in her handling (or lack thereof) of this situation. She decided to have a conversation Calvin to gain his insights about the Jake experience, as well as the current problem with Mitch.

Perhaps if Diane had coached Jake through the process, Calvin suggested, she might have discovered why the situation was so stressful for him; after all, Jake abandoned what could have been one of the greatest opportunities of his early career. Maybe Jake had such a fear of failure that he believed any setback, would reflect negatively on him, so he chose to remove himself from the situation, hoping to avoid continued conflict and possible failure. Further coaching from Diane might have helped Jake see the bigger picture perspective of the situation, and support him through resolving this uncomfortable setback. Diane recognized that she had been remiss in following through on her PACT with Jake to support him in his first leadership role.

And what about Mitch? One obstacle certainly was his strong hidden agenda. It appeared that he believed very deeply in his own idea and wanted a new module to his credit that would highlight his own professional skills and abilities. He may have been so focused on this need that he lost sight of what was most important for the organization. If Jake had taken the time during the early stages of the team's development to share this bigger picture perspective and discuss opportunities for alignment of personal goals and agendas with organizational goals, perhaps Mitch's needs for acknowledgement and advancement could have been identified and considered in a supportive, productive way. Unfortunately, Jake had not yet learned about the PACT'ing process.

This story illustrates some of the problems that can arise from personal fears, egos and hidden agendas. Additionally, it sadly demonstrates the lost opportunities when a clear *PACT* is not made, or when the *PACT* commitment is not followed through. This was one of those difficult leadership lessons for Diane. She made a commitment to herself to never again fall short on following up on any *PACT* she made.

Systematically Tending to "People Issues" as a Winning Formula

Health Assurance was a creative and insightful organization, so Jake's team wasn't the only Innovation Team set up—there were three others as well. Let's look at another scenario that had a more positive process and outcome.

Lilly was asked to lead the Pluto Innovation Team. Her team was charged with the same task as Jake's. Lilly told the team members that she believed the secret to their effectiveness as a team was for them to be supportive and honest with each other. Lilly said that her role was to facilitate this process and do her best to help ensure each individual's success, as well as that of the team.

In the early stages of team development, Lilly had the team members spend time getting to know one another and discussing their personal reasons for wanting to be on this team. They also shared what they felt they could contribute, as well as any fears or hesitations they had surrounding their own participation. Lilly believed this level of orientation was critical to the team building process, and an important first step in building trust. Her next step in building trust was to be very honest with the group and share her own personal agenda of hoping that this experience might help gain a promotion for her. She encouraged others to share any personal agendas, with the stated desire that the team could strive to support these individual professional goals while working towards organizational goals. Robert, the strategic planning partner on the team, said that he was concerned that his boss did not have a good sense of some of his capabilities. He was hoping this experience would demonstrate to his boss that he had strong marketing skills along with planning abilities. He wanted to transfer into marketing sometime down the road.

At the end of this meeting, all the team members agreed that they felt much more aligned as a team and much more understanding of each member.

Lilly's team went on to complete their project in half the time of Jake's. Certainly they ran into some obstacles along the way; however, their level of trust and honesty allowed them to more easily work through the disagreements they had. Here's an example. Robert seemed particularly edgy one day during a prioritization of projects meeting. He was pushing very hard on a project that required significant marketing efforts prior to development. This was not one of the more desirable projects based on the opportunity research. Lilly commented to Robert that he seemed a little out of sorts, and asked if there was anything the team could do. Robert explained that his boss had just given a special marketing planning project to someone else— someone with previous marketing experience—even though Robert had asked for the project. He was very disappointed. The team, being sensitive to Robert's goals in the marketing arena, made suggestions to appropriately expand the marketing efforts with both of the top priority projects. Such a shift benefited each of the projects and also supported Robert's personal goals for further marketing experience.

What was different with these two teams? Skill sets and experience were evenly matched; individual track records led to similar profiles for each member. How did one effectively and successfully develop a new product in a very short time period while the other did not? One significant difference: one leader used the *PACT* approach and the other did not. Other differences were primarily in the interpersonal skills sets and emotional strength of some of the team members. Success was a direct result of each person's ability—or inability—to manage difficult "people issues" in an effective way. The leaders' abilities in these same areas mattered most of all in setting up success or failure.

Leading People by Knowledge, Skill and Art

Leading people through these kinds of issues is not easy. As a matter of fact, it is probably the most difficult task of leadership. That is why there are so many ineffective teams, so much low productivity, so many dissatisfied employees, and so many bad bosses. Sure, there are often clear business, market and resource reasons for business downturns at times, and because they are clear, our bright and skilled folks can usually work through such challenges. It's the more subtle, emotional, human sides of people and how they interact in the workplace that is not always clear, that perplexes so many, and costs companies billions of dollars annually in decreased productivity and lost work time.

So, you might ask, do all leaders have to be psychologists or social workers to be effective? Do bosses have to spend all their time analyzing and counseling their employees, as opposed to planning and implementing business strategies? The answers to these questions are not simple. If you are one of those best bosses, you probably already have some insight into those deeper layers of human interactions and drivers and have learned some effective ways to work with them in achieving business success. And, the more we learn about the complexities of people, the more we realize there is still room to learn and grow as leaders.

For those who are new leaders and on an even steeper learning curve, welcome to the world of true leadership: the world where one of your key responsibilities is approaching your people and working with them as individuals with feelings, histories, a life outside the workplace, and needs based on complex experiences and situations.

So how do you get better at this? How do you help yourself and your people get along more effectively and humanely? As we said, this is not a simple task. It does come easier for some than others. Some of us have had the fortunate opportunities to have exemplary role models in mastery of human dynamics; some have had formal and informal training in the area; many are self-taught through reading, workshops, life experiences, and certainly the school of hard knocks. And then there are those who are in the really bad boss category, those who think they have this figured out, but, unfortunately, really haven't.

We believe the People*PACT* process and principles can help all of these bosses, as the art of human dynamics is a life long pursuit.

So far, we've talked about tending to the people, acknowledging their individual humanness as well as committing support to their growth, development and success. Treating people with respect and dignity is a fundamental part of this. Sounds simple, right? We grew up learning common rules of courtesy and respect. We learned about the concept of human dignity and treating all our fellow persons as equals... or did we? As a boss, it's time to do some deep soul searching and self-assessment to see how our values and beliefs impact our behavior relative to how we treat people.

It is beyond the scope of this book to walk you through such serious, in-depth self-reflection. However, it is our intention to help you understand the importance of self-reflection, self-awareness and self-regulation (later termed self-management). Daniel Goleman (1995) talks about this at length in his book *Emotional Intelligence.* Goleman performed groundbreaking brain and behavioral research and showed there are significant factors beyond IQ that impact individual leadership success. These factors define a different way of being smart; he calls it "emotional intelligence." Emotional intelligence includes self-awareness and impulse control, persistence, zeal and self-motivation, empathy and social deftness. He believes these factors are the common qualities to those who excel in life, be it at work or in personal relationships.

In his Harvard Business Review article on the topic, Goleman (1998, p. 76) defines self-awareness as "the ability to recognize and understand your moods, emotions, and drives, as well as their effect on others." He goes on to describe the hallmarks of self-awareness as: self-confidence, realistic self-assessment, and a self-deprecating sense of humor.

The second dimension of EI is the next step: self-management. Goleman (2002, p. 46) explains, "Self-management...is the component of emotional intelligence that frees us from being a prisoner of our feelings. It's what allows the mental clarity and concentrated energy that leadership demands, and what keeps disruptive emotions from throwing us off track." Goleman's hallmarks for self-management are: emotional self-control, transparency, adaptability, achievement, initiative and optimism.

We'll talk more about this in the chapter on perspective, as it is critical to your success as a leader. However, determining what might stand in your way of treating people with respect and dignity at all times is extremely important to consider. It is also important to recognize your behavior patterns around these issues. Do you raise your voice or yell at people? Do you talk down to people? Or perhaps you avoid emotional outbursts but have a tendency to ignore, interrupt, or discount people. Or maybe you are quick with sarcasm or zingers. Some of these you may do without even being aware of them. We can guarantee that how you treat people—respectfully or disrespectfully, dignified or not—significantly *impacts* your effectiveness as a leader. Check out Table 4.1 for additional examples of effective and ineffective/destructive behaviors in the bossing arena to get an idea of what works and what doesn't.

Does Your Past Get in the Way of Your Future?

Without having a strong belief in the dignity and respectful treatment of all human beings, it can be difficult to manage your behavior, especially those subtle, unconscious acts of disrespect. That's why understanding more about your core values and how they tie into your behaviors is important.

In the following story, we see how values, or in this case, prejudices, set long before the first day on the job, can significantly interfere with appropriate and effective behaviors in the workplace.

Harry was a manager in sales at Health Assurance. Joe was one of Harry's direct reports. Harry would often make negative comments to his fellow supervisors about Joe, criticizing his choice of friends, his car, his clothes, and even the way he talked. Harry rarely spoke directly to Joe, except to give petty criticisms about his work. (Joe, by the way, met or exceeded performance standards in all his job duties, according to the standard performance evaluation criteria of his job.) So why did Harry treat him with such disrespect? Finally, one of Harry's colleagues, our friend Diane, who formerly supervised Joe, mustered up the courage to ask him one day as they shared a beer after work. "Harry, you seem to be constantly on Joe's case. When he worked for me, his performance was fine, he was a good team player, and his co-workers liked him too. So, what's up with all your criticism?"

"I just don't like him," Harry snapped back.

Diane asked Harry, "So what is it about Joe you don't like?"

"I think he's basically a jerk," Harry replied. "He went to North High School, and all those guys were jerks."

"What made them jerks?" Diane asked. She could tell Harry seemed upset.

"They used to always drive by our school parking lot when we were getting off school on Fridays and throw trash at us, saying we would never amount to much because we went to West High School. It was really pretty ugly and hurtful to us then. I told myself that one day I would show them."

"Harry that must have been really painful for you as a teenager. Even now, it is still impacting you." Diane continued, now with a very empathetic tone, "Do you see that you are treating Joe differently than your other employees?"

"You know what Diane? You've got a point; I guess I really do come down harder on Joe than the other folks. I guess that's not really fair; he's really as good a performer as most." Harry said.

Diane, feeling comfortable with her long-time friend Harry and confident in her new crusade for coaching co-workers through authentic conversations, asked, "Do you think it's time to let go of that old stereotype and consider Joe as an individual, on his own merits?"

"Wow," Harry replied, "I had not realized that my old high school stereotypes were still with me twenty years later. A light bulb just went on for me. Thanks Diane."

Our past experiences and beliefs can *impact* our current behaviors, often times without us even realizing it. Harry was lucky to have a sensitive, experienced colleague like Diane, who was willing and skilled enough to walk him through this situation.

What can the rest of us do, who maybe don't have a "Diane" to help us out? Certainly, you can get feedback on how you act with employees—how you perform on the humane side of leadership. You can ask colleagues, ask your boss, and talk to your Human Resources folks about a 360-feedback process where you can receive anonymous information from people at work about your effectiveness as a leader. You can utilize the services of an executive coach.

You can also look at how your team performs, and how they relate to you. Are they comfortable bringing their problems to you and seeking your advice? Or do they only bring the good news? Do you have relaxed, friendly, casual conversations, or are they stiff and reserved around you? Regardless of how justified you may feel in your approach to management, analyzing the way your employees be-have around you can help you decide whether you need to change certain behaviors. This is the "self-management" part.

As you become more and more aware of your behaviors, you can also control those behaviors more effectively and choose to act in ways that are more respectful and more humane. Table 4.1. lists behaviors that support this type of humane treatment of people, as well as behaviors that don't support humane treatment. Please read these and consider how well and how often you practice these be-haviors. For example:

- Do you always treat everyone with the utmost respect and dignity?
- Do you always tend to the people first, and trust they will get the work done?
- What efforts have you taken to drive fear out of the workplace? (See Chapter 8)
- Do you keep humor in the work place?
- Have you created a safe environment for risk taking and creativity?
- Do you treat everyone fairly?
- Do you communicate clearly and honestly? (More about how to do this as we go on.)

In summary, being one of the best bosses has a lot to do with how you treat your people. It's about being fully committed to supporting them in doing the best job they possibly can. It's all about how you see your job as being the supporter, the coach and resource finder for employees. And it's about believing in and demonstrating your belief in the value of each individual human being, and the contribution they can make through making the *PACT*.

TABLE 4.1. Behaviors That Work, Behaviors That Don't Work

Listed below are a number of "bossing behaviors" that are commonly seen in the workplace. We have identified examples of results that are encouraged or promoted by each of these behaviors. These results can show up in terms of company culture, workplace atmosphere and behavior norms. Because the boss' behavior is carefully scrutinized and is often adopted by employees it is critical that leaders consider their behaviors for the consequences they may bring.

Behaviors that work	Promotes:	Behaviors that don't work	Promotes:
Praising people often and sincerely for specific reasons	Growth	Praising employees rarely	Resentment
Treating people well	Generosity	Playing Favorites	Jealousy
Treating people as individuals	Pride	Treating everyone the same	Frustration
Telling the truth with compassion	Understanding	Telling the truth bluntly	Hurt and Anger
Being an excellent role model	Consistency	"Do as I say, not as I do" role model	Dishonesty
Thinking carefully before responding in a tense situation	Rationality	Snapping back an answer immediately, especially in anger	Fear and Resentment
Remaining calm	Respect	Shouting, slamming doors	Hostility or Fear
Having fun, maintaining humor	Lightness and Balance	Teasing, inappropriate jokes, zingers or humor at other's expense	Pain and Lawsuits
Admitting mistakes and saying you are sorry	Kindness and Respect	Insisting you are right no matter what	Stubbornness
Being friendly	Warmth	Being flirty	Harassment
Being scrupulously careful about employees confidential information	Trustworthiness	Sharing personal information about employees	Distrust

Behaviors that work	Promotes:	Behaviors that don't work	Promotes:
Being fair about rewards, raises and promotions	Credibility	Letting personal feelings influence pay and promotions	Arbitrariness and resentment
Being supportive and understanding when employees are stressed	Empathy	Giving unsolicited advice or judging others troubles	Arrogance and Secrecy
Motivating employees to do their best through support, rewards & praise	Support	Intimidating employees into doing better by creating a fearful environment	Oppression and Alienation
Providing the big picture to increase understanding and sound thinking	Strategic Thinking and Trust	Minimal communication and lack of information sharing	Discounted
Knowing the end, never justifies the means	Strong Principles	Thinking you can violate a rule or someone's trust	Disrespect and Distrust
Being flexible when appropriate	Creativity and Loyalty	Unwilling to try to find a solution to an employee's problem	Rigidity and Resentment
Clarifying every communication, especially the surprising ones	Understanding and Trust	Jumping to conclusions, following mis-assumptions	Poor Communication
Appreciating each person's unique contribution	Diversity and Harmony	Thinking everyone should be the same or like you	Narrow-mindedness and Conflict
Speaking to people privately about sensitive issues	Sensitivity	Giving criticism or sensitive information in front of others	Insensitivity and Cruelty
Helping employees to settle disputes quickly AND with guidance	Productivity and Harmony	Leaving it up to employees to "work out" their differences, abandonment	Avoidance and Cowardice
Making rules known, alerting people early and clarifying consequences	Fairness	Surprising people with negative consequences or dismissal	Vindictiveness and Litigation

Chapter 5
PERSPECTIVE
FILLING IN THE GAPS

"Understanding is the beginning of approving."

— *Andre Gide*

How the Big Picture Brings Greater Understanding

The Big Picture

While there are many ways to support people, one of the most underrated is providing them with perspective. Without the "bigger picture" it is nearly impossible to do much more than follow very simple and precise directions in a routine fashion. In our new service economy, employees are often called upon to make decisions about their jobs and customer needs. The more an employee knows about the big picture (the vision, the business, the process and policy), the better their decisions and contributions can be.

Vision

It would be very difficult to create a strong *PACT* without clear understanding of the vision/strategy of the organization and how the team/department's work fits in and contributes to that strategy. Individuals work much more effectively and with greater job satisfaction when they understand how their individual contribution fits in the larger context of the team and the full organization.

Great leaders keep their people focused on a compelling vision. This can be the vision of the organization, or that of their individual team, but it must function as the home base for employees to return when they lose focus. Such lost focus can lead to decreased productivity, confusion, unhappiness, chaos...need we go on? The key impact of a compelling vision is alignment. When people are aligned behind a vision, this can serve as the light at the end of the tunnel in trying times and keep them from being pulled in too many directions or having conflict over good, but incompatible, ideas. Knowing that they are working towards an ultimate goal through a shared vision creates an inspiring environment and a motivated, successful team.

The vision also sets the course for the planning process. Great leaders know how to maximize the planning process and use it to keep their team's effort focused and guided. A solid, practical plan can serve as a great tool for offering the bigger picture perspective. Good bosses know how to develop and manage a plan to achieve their desired outcomes, as well as use it as a touchstone for bringing perspective to their people.

A strong leader uses that compelling vision and plan to help people develop individual goals, tactics and performance measurements that align with the vision and plan. This, in turn, helps support the leader's responsibility of balancing the needs of the organization with the needs of the individuals and teams within the organization.

Bringing Perspective

What does it take to share this accurate big picture perspective with the people around us? Helping people understand crucial issues and enabling them to see the need for complete and accurate information is an exceptional leadership skill.

After you have established a fairly solid big picture perspective for yourself, you need to discover how to help others see an accurate big picture. We will highlight the most crucial elements and encourage you to learn more about each.

Keys to Bringing Perspective:

There are five key elements involved in the big picture perspective and how you share it with someone else:

1. Self-Awareness
2. Effective Communication and "Fact vs Fiction"
3. Information Gathering and Learning
4. Understanding Others and Diversity of Thinking
5. Balance

1. Self-Awareness

Before you can bring an accurate big picture perspective to your people you must gain such a perspective for yourself. To do this, you need a solid perspective of yourself—your beliefs and values systems, your emotions in the

workplace, your leadership style, and the impact your behavior has on others.

Daniel Goleman (1995, p. 47), creator of the Emotional
Intelligence ("EQ") model, calls this "self-awareness."

"...awareness of one's own feelings as they occur....is
the fundamental emotional competence on which others
(competencies), such as emotional self-control, build."

Goleman (1995, 2002) has laid the groundwork for the
now highly accepted concept that Emotional Intelligence,
or EQ, is a better predictor of leadership success than IQ.
As a boss, your emotions and behaviors probably have a
far greater impact on people than you ever imagined. It
is critical for a leader to be keenly aware of her feelings,
emotions, and behavior. It is also critical to be aware of
and sensitive to the impact your behavior has on those
around you. This level of self-awareness is your first step
to bringing perspective.

Positional Power: Let's take a moment here to discuss a
phenomenon that ties into the boss's self-awareness: positional power. We have heard bosses say, "I just don't get it,
I get this promotion, and I'm still the same person I always
was, but people are treating me differently...they don't
come up and talk to me like they used to, they seem much
more stand-offish, or at least less candid, almost afraid..."
This is a classic demonstration of employees' reaction to
their perception of positional power.

It comes with the territory of being a boss, and it requires
deep self-awareness to keep this perception of power from
becoming an obstacle in leadership.

Here's an example of a time when self-awareness and
appreciation of the potential intimidation of positional

power could have helped a manager avoid significant stress between two team members:

One of Diane's greatest joys in her leadership role was mentoring aspiring new leaders. She was now well versed in the need for self-awareness and the challenges of the phenomenon of positional power. She found one of the best ways to teach her new leaders about this was through recounting the following story about her days as a new leader...

Diane, Mark and Jeri had worked on the same team for five years. When Diane earned her promotion, she was suddenly Mark and Jeri's boss. One day during a staff meeting, Mark and Jeri were presenting a proposal on a project they had focused on for the past six months. They believed this project could be a tremendous enhancement for customer service.

Diane had just come from her boss Murray's staff meeting, where he had criticized his entire team for recent low ratings on customer service. Although Diane was upset at how condescending Murray had been to the team, she was still excited to hear Mark and Jeri's proposal, hoping it might offer an opportunity for turnaround for the company. Diane had full faith in Mark and Jeri's capabilities and believed if anyone could create a new way of delivering their services, they were the ones!

So, during their presentation, Diane listened intently—even more so than normal. She was not instilling her usual light-heartedness into the discussion. This was a critical time for the organization, and she needed to help develop a solution. Near the end of the presentation, Diane had a problem with one of her contact lenses. She tried not to distract from Mark's "grand finale closing," but her focus was clearly compromised. Then Murray came barging through the door and demanded Diane to come immediately to his office.

She made a quick "thank you, great job, we'll talk more about this tomorrow..." comment, and hurried to Murray's office.

Now, left behind were Mark and Jeri, devastated in the wake of this, all because of their interpretation—or in this case, misinterpretation—of Diane's reaction to their presentation.

Mark was clearly disappointed. "Wow, Diane didn't seem impressed at all!"

Jeri agreed. "You're right...she hardly said a word."

"Did you see her grimacing at my final overheads? I thought those were the best ideas of all!" Mark sighed.

Jeri: "And what about Murray barging in like that?!"

Mark: "What a jerk; he didn't even say excuse me!"

So, here's the result of this comedy of errors. Mark and Jeri are demoralized, thinking their boss hated their proposal and rejected their hard work, and they go home that night thinking their great ideas are in the toilet. If only Diane had been more aware of the fact that when you're the boss, people watch you more intently, and interpret (or misinterpret) your body language in all sorts of ways. If Diane had known this, she might have been more aware of her body language and explained her grimacing was the result of her contact irritating her eye and not a look of disapproval.

And, if only Murray had apologized for the interruption and explained that there was an urgent matter that needed immediate attention. In truth, there was: his father had just had a heart attack. He needed to brief Diane, as he was leaving her in charge during his absence.

If Diane had been more aware of the impact of her subtle behavior and explained it (which would have taken only a few seconds!), Mark and Jeri could have gone home that night feeling great about all their hard work; instead they felt horrible.

Imagine how their moods impacted their families when they got home...but that's a story for another day.

Although there are many lessons for better bossing in this story, we're focused on the importance of self-awareness. Be cognizant of the power your position holds in the minds of your people. Your employees scrutinize everything you do or say. They can easily misinterpret your body language, tone of voice, as well as your comments. Watch it, manage it, and explain it, if need be.

Be aware of your behavior, particularly if it is out of your norm. Explain what it is that is causing you to be more serious, quiet and/or questioning than usual.

One final note on self-awareness: great leaders always consider their intention behind their words and actions and ensure that they are well meaning. In the workplace, this includes balancing what's best for the individual with what's best for the organization—taking the full picture perspective into consideration. Having a deep level of self-awareness includes being aware of your underlying intentions. And remember, successful leaders, great leaders, operate at the highest level of integrity, having truly good intentions at heart.

> ### Asking Questions
> When you question, especially if you ask a lot of questions, clarify your intention. Sometimes people assume that your questions are intended to find fault in their work. Clarification of your intention is the key: for example, "I know I'm asking a lot of questions. This is a very important issue, and I think you may have a great idea here for resolution. So I really want to understand it as thoroughly as possible. That way, I can more fully support you in achieving what you want to do."
>
> Sometimes questions from the boss put people on the defensive. This can be strongly influenced by how the question is phrased, tone of voice, or even choice of words. For example, we suggest doing your best to avoid the word "why", as it typically puts people on the defense. Instead of saying, "Why did you do that?" consider saying, "I'd like to better understand your thinking behind what you have done. Let's talk about it more."
>
> Check out your own intentions for asking the question. Are you truly trying to support the individual? Are you seeking more complete understanding? Keep checking out your own internal drivers—great bosses certainly do!

2. Effective Communication & "Fact vs Fiction"

As we stress throughout this book, good communication goes hand-in-hand with good leadership. It is rare that one can provide too much good communication. Quality, as well as quantity, makes for good communication. And, stellar communication is fundamental to a successful *PACT* process.

Fact vs Fiction, or "I thought you said..." One of the core elements of communication is understanding the difference between fact and fiction. As leaders attempt to gather and share more complete information, it is critical to understand the difference between objective data, opinion and rumor.

In their book *Play to Win!*, Larry and Hirsh Wilson (1998) define the phenomenon of "MSU" or "making stuff up." Frequently we are unaware that some of what we are thinking is fabricated rather than fact. The Wilsons explain how most of our current beliefs, reactions and behaviors are based on our past experiences. Most of these experiences did not include the full picture of objective information or fact either.

> ...We have created meaning—inaccurate and incomplete—out of these (current events) and a million other events in our lives. We don't think about them anymore, we don't hold them up to the light and think, 'Gee, what did I make up about not being picked to play?' They simply operate unchallenged (Wilson, 1998, p. 77).

They operate unchallenged and become incorporated into what we *perceive* as the "truth." For example, what one might "make up" about not being selected for a team is that they are not popular. This may not be the reason at all they were not picked to play, however, they move forward, believing and acting as if they are not popular. Unfortunately, our perceptions do not always provide us with the full picture.

The following story illustrates the way our assumptions ("MSU") can affect our version of "reality."

It is a dreary Monday morning, and Diane has just had a long commute into the office in very heavy traffic. As she enters the parking lot she sees her new boss Calvin speeding away with a very intent look on his face. As she comes through the front door, the receptionist Betty says, "Have you heard the news? They are saying that Calvin was just fired and the rumor is that there will be at least 100 people laid off. Can you believe it?" Diane advises Betty not to panic; since she is one of the longest-tenured employees, her job is safe. Diane lets Betty know that she will be back later to give her more information as she gets it.

Down the hall, she sees another manager, Jack Smith, with his head down, in a deep and seemingly distressing phone conversation. As she rounds the corner to her office, she encounters one of her analysts. "Hi, Bob. How are you today?" Bob replies, "How good can I be? I guess I will be one of the first to go. They always let the new guys go first. With a new baby on the way, things will be pretty tight for Janet and me."

Diane begins to worry seriously herself.

Diane no sooner walked into her office than her phone began ringing. It was Calvin, calling from his cell phone.

"Hi Diane," he said in an almost breathless tone, "I had to rush down to Health Reliance. We just got the word that our merger with them is moving forward, and before we could begin implementation of the communication plan, word got out in their ranks. The rumor on the street is that the merger will drive lay-offs of up to 100 of their employees. They asked me to come down and help set up employee support

processes because these lay-off rumors require some serious damage control. I just wanted to give you a heads up as to what was going on; you know how the rumor mill can be. Please be assured this will have no direct impact on any jobs at Health Assurance, just in case the rumor has gotten convoluted over there. I'll give you a call later today with an update and a solid communication plan for our Health Assurance folks about this situation."

Diane hung up the phone relieved...but also embarrassed. How quickly she had assumed the worst and even contributed to the rumor mill by not discouraging the rumors on the basis of lack of objective data.

How many times have we reacted on "made up stuff"? Think of the damage Diane could do as a leader of the company perpetuating such rumors without all the facts. The moral to this story is to gather as much objective and complete information as possible, so we, or others, don't have to fill in the gaps with made up stuff. Thus we can have a greater understanding of a situation, and hopefully, respond more appropriately.

Even though the phenomenon of MSU is extremely common and often unconscious we can take steps to ensure that it doesn't cause big roadblocks.

- Awareness of the process is the first step. Ask yourself, "Is what I'm thinking and basing this decision or action on objective data, or is it made up stuff?
- This thinking can lead to a new level of awareness and sensitivity to seeking more complete and accurate information.
- You can then start framing certain comments with, "The actual facts I have on this issue are... What I'm

making up about this is..."

When we consciously strive to separate fact from fiction and check out our assumptions, life and work become simpler.

Didn't you mean... Effective listening is another way to check out your assumptions. We're not talking about "active listening" here, that concept so many of us learned in Communications 101, where one merely regurgitates what they just heard the speaker saying. Rather, we're talking about listening with the intention to truly understand where the other person is coming from: the art of setting aside your own opinions and listening in such a way as to more fully understand the other person's perspective. Stephen Covey (2004, p. 192) calls this empathetic listening:

> To truly listen means to transcend your own autobiography, to get out of your frame of reference, out of your own value system, out of your own history and judging tendencies, and to get deeply into the frame of reference or viewpoint of another person.

A common mistake in the listening process is to get caught up in one's own thoughts, to begin to develop your argument in support of or in disagreement with the speaker's. How can we be fully listening to someone, let alone attempting to understand where they are coming from, if we are busy developing our own rebuttal while they are speaking? Listening for understanding is about being aware of our internal conversations during the act of listening, and then checking out our "made-up-stuff" after the speaker has finished. By allowing the speaker to clarify what he meant, you address your own assumptions and either gain a better understanding or hear a magic phrase from them: "Yes! That's exactly what I meant." Either way, you can bet they felt that they were heard.

People want and need to be heard accurately. The ability to facilitate this process is a true gift that good bosses can offer their people. Greater communication brings greater understanding of the bigger picture perspective and a more effective *PACT*.

3. Information Gathering & Learning

One of the ways a boss can help bring the bigger picture perspective is to provide as much relevant and accurate information as possible. This starts with the highest level of the picture—the organization's vision and strategies—and includes objective data, as well as the range of opinions on the subject. Try to quantify and qualify this information, so that a fuller, realistic picture begins to emerge. Take a look at two different scenarios related to the same piece of information and see the difference in the outcome when more background information was provided.

> *Health Alliance's executive leadership team met to discuss replacing the current computer system. Calvin explained that many of their operating costs, especially drugs and medical equipment, had increased more that year than expected, and that the increased expenses were equivalent to the cost of the proposed new computer system. The team discussed the pros and cons of delaying the IT system replacement by one year, and felt that, overall, a delay would not have any negative impact in productivity or quality. It also would be better than cutting salary increases, which*

was the only other possible area for cuts. Bottom-line, the group agreed to delay purchasing the new information technology system for one year.

Ryan, a classic command and control boss, went back to his group and announced there would not be any computer upgrades until next year—end of story. His group was very upset, particularly since Ryan had talked up this state-of-the-art upgrade as a great benefit for them. His people spent the rest of the day talking about how cheap the organization was, how they didn't care about providing the best for the people, and all sorts of other made-up-stuff.

Diane went back from executive staff meeting to her group and shared the same announcement about the delay of new computers. Unlike Ryan, she shared with her team the highlights of the discussion from executive staff: the increased expense of materials, the pros and cons of delaying the computer purchase and the other option of decreased raises. Diane painted a much more complete picture of the issue and the decision. Although her team was disappointed, they better understood the issues involved in this decision, and did not get all worked up about the made-up-stuff that cost Ryan's team the rest of the day.

The same announcement but different levels of explanation or perspective setting, and look at the difference in outcomes. Diane took less than ten minutes to summarize the meeting discussion, and her staff went on to have a productive day. Ryan's staff did not have a productive day. Does providing more information help? You bet it does—it helps create a more relevant *PACT*, and it even impacts the bottom line!

4. Understanding Others and Diversity of Thinking

To better gain the full picture perspective, it is important to have a reasonable level of understanding of the people involved. This includes understanding their goals, their perspective and opinion on the issue, and their experience. This knowledge enhances understanding of all the elements involved in the issue, which in turn, enhances the breadth and depth of the picture of understanding that is being painted. Sometimes people look and sound as though they are in agreement, while a deeper understanding of their needs and issues can reveal that they have differences. Over time these differences can diverge direction and goals. This can be avoided by spending the time early on to explore people's opinions and core motivations, and then finding ways to blend, combine or negotiate those differences into consensus.

Inclusivity is important to developing the big picture. This process encourages the sharing and consideration of differences. These differences can be differences in thinking styles, opinion, experience, culture, backgrounds, or gender. Encouraging such inclusiveness, such diversity, certainly helps to enrich the perspective on any issue, and always leads to greater understanding and appreciation. If people are excluded in ways that are fundamentally important to them, they are compelled to find recourse, which is often disruptive.

Much has been written on the issue of diversity. Our key points here focus on maximizing the learnings, creativity and innovation that can come from diverse experience and thinking. When making a *PACT*, the great boss knows to encourage their team members to share their ideas and opinions, and help the individuals increase their own level of self-awareness regarding how their thinking aligns with that of others on the team and with the organization. Are they in close alignment, or is their thinking on the fringes? Then, the innovative boss tries to discern if the fringe thinkers are true innovators or if they are saboteurs, or maybe just not fully informed. In making the *PACT*, encouraging this diversity of thinking can truly bring about innovation, as well as help increase employees' level of self-awareness.

5. Balance

Balance in your work life, both between the different components of work, as well as between work and home, not only helps to bring the big picture perspective to others, such balance is the bigger picture. A boss who creates balance in the workplace through modeling and supporting others in balancing provides one of the best support functions possible to maintain a healthy work environment.

Balancing work components through prioritization of core job responsibilities is an important place to start. As a good boss, you do this both for yourself and for those working for you. Such balancing and priority setting for leaders is critical, otherwise the all-too-common problem of getting caught up in what's urgent, versus what's important, begins to reek havoc on accomplishing goals. A common mistake many bosses make is not setting "leading and supporting my people" as a top priority. This often gets shoved down to the bottom of the list, if it ever appears at all. We contend that leading your people, supporting them in doing the best job they can do, is one of the highest priorities for any manager. Don't get so caught up with all the actions on your "To Do List" that you don't take the time to tend to your people; in the long run, you will decrease productivity and quality of output—both yours and theirs—if you do not attend to your responsibilities of leadership.

Now, for balancing and prioritizing the remainder of your responsibilities, let your job description and your plan (or annual goals and objectives) drive your core priorities. Keeping a balance here will absolutely not only help you be more effective and successful, you will also be serving as an excellent role model for your team. Then, in the *PACT'*ing process, helping team members set their work priorities in a similar way will also help them keep focus and balance at work.

Do As You Say

Modeling the balance between work and home (home here means any interests outside work) is a very important way for the boss to "walk the talk." If you tell your people it is important to balance and not take work home, you need to do that as well. If they continue to get voicemails or emails from you at midnight (and don't kid yourself – they check those time and date stamps!) you will be sending a mixed message. Do they do what you say or do what you do?! A tough choice for many, but usually "do what you do" wins out.

Taking regular time away from work is critical for good health: physical, psychological, and spiritual. And if people are not healthy, they cannot sustain the high performance that will bring about the breakthrough results you are hoping to achieve. Bring the perspective of balance to your people through your talk and your walk.

This helps paint the biggest picture perspective. It isn't all just about work...it's about making it all fit together: work, family, friends, community, health and spirit. Imagine how supported your people could feel if they knew they had a boss who sincerely cared and operated in a way that helps to maintain a balance while creating a winning environment for everyone.

See how you can work this into the PACT!

Chapter 6
ACKNOWLEDGEMENT & FEEDBACK

"Don't find fault. Find a remedy."

— *Henry Ford*

How Praise and Feedback Enhance Performance

Acknowledgement in business management is used most commonly as a form of positive reinforcement, recognition and/ or rewards. *Feedback* is more often associated with constructive comments or criticism, however can also include the positive side as well. Acknowledgement and feedback are essential to the growth, improvement and well-being of any employee or business. They are crucial to the work environment where everyone is learning, teaching or changing most of the time. In this chapter we are going to look at each of these terms in the way they are most commonly perceived in the workplace.

The *PACT'*ing boss knows that acknowledgement is the simplest and least expensive way to help people stay motivated. Frequent, sincere acknowledgement is one of the most effective ways you can positively impact the performance and behavior of people, **and** it costs nothing. Research shows that people grow through strength and confidence building, and a good leader encourages growth at every opportunity (Branham, 2005).

A report from an American Express Incentive Services survey of 1,002 full-and part-time employees conducted by Washington, D.C. based research firm Wirthlin Worldwide (Grimaldi, 2000) was summarized as follows:

- Ninety-two percent of respondents said being motivated is important to their job performance, and ninety-two percent said it is a key factor in their loyalty to the firm.
- More than three quarters of those surveyed said their boss's appreciation is a factor in keeping them on the job: seventy-eight percent said they were likely to be working for the same company for the next two years, based on the current level of motivation they receive from their bosses.
- More than half reported that their bosses verbally recognized or thanked them. Twenty-nine percent said their managers used incentive programs and rewards, and twenty-six percent cited promotions and raises. Sixty-five percent of the respondents whose companies offered structured incentives said those programs provided ongoing motivation.

Let's look at a story that illustrates the impact that acknowledgement, or lack thereof, can have on individuals as well as an organization.

Rick was a supervisor in the Customer Service department of Health Assurance. He had held his position for eight years and was generally satisfied with his job and the company. Health Assurance was happy with him as well. Rick's department continually received high ratings on customer surveys and his employee turnover rate was 75% lower than the average for the company. Each year the company showed their appreciation of Rick by providing him the highest merit increase allowed by policy. As Rick's supervisor, Diane was a great role model who routinely offered positive acknowledgements, as well as helpful suggestions for improvement. Last year, Customer Service was moved from Marketing into the Sales area, and Rick got a new boss, Pat.

Although Rick knew he would miss Diane as a boss, as they had developed a great, trusting relationship, he was pleased to have Pat in the position. They had worked together on various teams over the years, and Rick knew Pat to be concerned with customer service and a person of great integrity. Nothing seemed to change much with Pat at the helm: Rick's department turnover stayed the same; customer feedback was still outstanding; Rick even received the highest merit increase again. However, Rick felt like something was different: while he had trouble putting his finger on it at first, he realized it one day when he was complimenting one of his employees on a job well done. Rick received no feedback or acknowledgement, on a personal level, from Pat. Sure, Pat had given him a great raise and reviewed the customer survey annual report with him, but Pat had never once mentioned his appreciation for Rick's work or efforts. Rick could not recall a single time in the last year that Pat made any comments regarding how he felt about Rick's work. The result was powerful: for the first time in seven years, Rick did not look forward to going to work each day. Rick considered himself a stable, confident individual, and he was rather surprised to find how strongly this lack of recognition had impacted him.

Before this epiphany, Rick was seriously thinking about looking for a new job with a different company, thinking maybe he had just burnt out. He realized that this lack of acknowledgement was not only an issue for him, but had also impacted other parts of the sales division since his boss was the VP of Sales. His colleagues had been complaining that their workplace "just didn't seem to have the spirit that it used to... People just don't seem as motivated....morale seems down." In fact, the turnover rate for this division had increased in the last year. Rick decided to go to his employee development partner in HR to talk about ways to improve the level of personal acknowledgment in the entire division.

Wouldn't it be great if all managers were as insightful as Rick and willing to try to appropriately improve situations? Unfortunately, there are too many cases when, rather than attempting to effect change and improvement from within, people just leave. This story clearly illustrates how acknowledgement can have significant impact to both culture and the bottom-line, because of the high cost of turnover.

Acknowledgement
It's Worth the Effort

What do we mean by acknowledgement? Does it mean we nod our head when someone walks into the room? Does it mean we compliment someone when they perform their basic job duties satisfactorily? Is acknowledgement when we give someone an award for outstanding performance? We contend that acknowledgement is all of this and more.

Simply speaking, what we mean by acknowledgement is any time that you positively recognize someone for who they are or what they have done. So, looking at the examples above, when we nod our head, or smile or greet someone who walks in the room, we are affirming to them that we notice and appreciate they are present. When we compliment someone on his work, we are letting him know that we notice and value his efforts. And certainly, when we reward someone for something he has done well, we are recognizing his contributions and skills. All of these gestures are recognition and acknowledgement, and all are very important ways of supporting people and establishing an environment that is conducive to self-motivation.

As a matter of fact, we contend that the type of acknowledgment made—whether a simple nod or something as large as a multi-thousand dollar bonus—is not as important as the actual act of acknowledgement itself. And at the core of the art of acknowledgement are three fundamental aspects: *sincerity, specificity and frequency.* Remembering and applying these make the difference between an employee/boss relationship that works and one that doesn't. (Note: you can use this at home also.)

Sincerity

You must be sincere when you offer any type of acknowledgement. You must believe in the value of this person and/or her work, and appreciate the specific aspect you are recognizing. Your intention and your words must be honest; people sense insincerity, and without this crucial element you run the risk of causing more damage than good.

The trick here involves the old adage "Catch them doing something right." Everyone does something well. When you observe, either directly or through other's reports of good work that someone has done, let that person know you know about it and how much you appreciate it.

The words "thank you" have a tremendous impact as well, when said sincerely.

Specificity

It is also important to be specific about the individual's actions or behaviors, and the value you see in them. When you provide a concrete example of the behavior or quality you are complimenting, it helps the individual better understand your intention, as well as her own strengths. Furthermore, when you add your belief in the value of an employee's behavior, it further reinforces development and growth—both for the individual as well as the organization. Research shows that individuals repeat behaviors that are positively reinforced.

Simply saying something like, "You're doing a great job, Jan," doesn't have nearly the impact as, "Jan, you did a terrific job in handling the patient in room 101 today who was upset with her long wait on the doctor. You not only skillfully calmed her down with your great listening, but you also had her laughing in the end. She left the building singing our praises. That is truly the kind of personalized customer care we are trying to promote here; thanks for being such a great role model for your colleagues!" That's what we mean by specificity.

Frequency

To maximize the power that appropriate acknowledgment can bring to an individual's growth and motivation, we believe that frequent doses, even if small, are in most cases, more effective than very infrequent, large doses. One caution here however, is to not get so caught up in the frequency mode that you lose the sincerity and specificity components of the acknowledgement equation. First be genuine and explicit about their good work, then make sure you do it often enough that your team members feel confident in knowing their boss truly recognizes their talents and efforts.

If you are following the People*PACT* process of *Performance Support*, your ongoing informal meetings with your employees offers the perfect opportunity to provide specific acknowledgement of good work. And, if you are having these meetings regularly as we suggest, the frequency factor is covered as well. Make it a point to always close those meetings with a specific compliment to the employee.

Categories of Acknowledgement

In her book, *The Four-Fold Way*, anthropologist Angeles Arrian (1993) describes how people throughout the world acknowledge each other in four fundamental ways. All four are equally important to the development of solid self-image and confidence. Arrien explains, "Wherever we receive the least acknowledgement is where we may carry a belief of inadequacy or low self-esteem" (1993, p. 49).

This concept of acknowledgement can be adapted to the workplace, where acknowledgement serves as one of the most, if not the most, effective tool for motivation. A complete program of acknowledgement will help to support the most well-rounded skills sets and abilities in employees.

The categories of acknowledgement that Arian describes are:
- Physical Appearance
- Skills
- Character qualities
- Impact we make on each other

Here are some examples of appropriate acknowledgements for the workplace in each category:

Physical/Appearance
- *Jack, I really like that tie. The design is very contemporary and colorful.*
- *Mary, is that a new picture of your sons? They are really growing up, and so handsomely!*
- *Kate, I think that new picture you just hung in your office looks great in there. I really like the colors and design.*
- *Jack...got a new jacket? I like that longer length cut!*

Skill
- *Jane, you did a fantastic job setting up that spreadsheet. I know it was very complicated with a lot of formulas. I want you to know I was not only impressed by the quality of your work, but also by how quickly you turned*

it around. It helped me get the information to our customer one day ahead of schedule. Thanks!

- *Mike, I was truly impressed by how well you handled that irate customer. He started out yelling and ended up walking out happy, thanks to how carefully you listened to his issue and patiently worked out a very reasonable resolution that worked for him AND us. Way to go!*

- *Jake, I just want you to know that this draft contract you typed·was perfect! Not only were there no typos in all 25 pages, you also skillfully interpreted all our redlines and write-ins. You did an outstanding job with this! I believe your work helped us get the contract signed more quickly, which meant more business sooner for us! Thank you very much.*

- *Laura, I want you to know how much I appreciate how well you handle our very busy switchboard. I have seen you manage multiple in-coming calls with grace and professionalism. Also, our phone reports indicate that you are well above our standards for number of rings till answer, and number of holds, AND your average hold time is only ten seconds, one third our standard! That is great support for our customer service strategy. I truly appreciate your tremendous effort!*

Character Qualities

- *Jan, you have a great sense of humor. I always appreciate how you can find fun in even some of the most trying times. Like the other day when you laughed after I informed the team that our quotas were increased again. Your comment that "they know who to go to for help!" broke the tension and gave others a positive way to look at this challenging situation.*

- *Tom, I so appreciate your positive attitude, and how your sharing of that with others can often be very helpful in problem solving. Like yesterday during the meeting, when everyone was caught up in how the budget cuts were going to limit our business travel to out-of-town customers, you immediately not only came up with great suggestions around virtual customer calls, but also reminded everyone of how the decreased travel was going to allow everyone to spend more time with their families—something everyone values! I believe your perspective helped to shift the direction of the meeting toward a positive outcome. I am grateful for your ability and willingness to share those great positive spins!*

Impact on Others

- *Mike, it is amazing to watch how your high energy and upbeat nature seem to brighten up the team when you walk in the room! We have a tough year facing us and you help give the team members confidence in themselves. I really appreciate the positive impact that you have on the mood of our team meetings.*
- *Mary, the way you are able to get everyone on the team engaged in our discussions is outstanding. You have made a tremendous impact on the cohesiveness of this team since you joined. Thank you very much.*
- *Bob, you always find the high road to take in any conflict that comes up within the team. Your leadership and example of maturity inspires others on the team to the same high level of behavior and attitude. Thank you for the impact that has on our experience and the great results it helps us achieve.*

Public or Private—Pros and Cons

Despite instincts that might move leaders to reward employees in public settings, we have found that the most effective and most impactful method of acknowledgement is provided in private, one-on-one conversations.

Certainly many people disagree: consider how many companies celebrate individual success ceremonially. And who wouldn't want to have their names read by a company executive at a large gathering? (Actually, lots of people!) And what co-worker wouldn't feel great satisfaction in watching his teammate honored? (Sadly, quite a few!) The truth is, plenty of people don't want the attention, and others aren't interested in the animosity or resentment that might come with the "honor." The individual, private venue is the *most effective* method for the long run; you can't go wrong with individual, private acknowledgement, delivered as we have described above. It gives you the chance to be very thorough and specific. It lets you ask questions and tell the individual each aspect of your appreciation for their good work. It also gives the recipient a private moment to bask in the acknowledgement without the self-consciousness that can come in front of others.

Although public acknowledgement can have its appropriate place, there are many potential pitfalls on that road, and one must be very mindful of all the potential implications if you lean towards more public acknowledgement. Here are a few risks:

- It can foster unhealthy competition within teams or work groups;
- Public award programs that only recognize one or a few individuals or teams often leave the others feeling as

if they have done nothing worthwhile. This of course is the antithesis to the whole meaning and intention around acknowledgement;

- Non-recognized individuals may feel that they have achieved similar accomplishments but have not been rewarded. Unfortunately, they may be correct; we can't always know about all the great deeds our folks do, nor are we able to reasonably keep track of them all. Therefore, public acknowledgement brings such imperfections in tracking to the front page;
- Some individuals are uncomfortable with public recognition;
- It is only feasible to do so much of this type of acknowledgement, and you therefore miss the need for frequency if the public venue is your principal method of delivery.

How to Wisely Use Public Acknowledgement

One method of providing individual acknowledgement publicly can be tied in with individual's special work anniversaries, such as one year, five year, ten year, etc. You can certainly be consistent with this: everyone knows it is fair and provided to everyone equally, and it can provide a great opportunity to acknowledge individual skills, characteristics and accomplishments for others to witness and celebrate.

If you use public acknowledgement, solicit stories, nominations, and endorsements from others on the team since you will then be able to have a much more comprehensive and accurate view of everyone's accomplishments.

Customize and Personalize
as Much as Possible

We have already shared the importance of sincerity, specificity and frequency. Another aspect to this "art form" is the value of personalizing your methodology and rewards to the needs and wants of the individual. In other words, talk to your employees. Check out what they want—what floats their boat! It can be different for each individual. If you want to go beyond the realm of verbal or written acknowledgement described above, you could consider the following. Particularly in the area of rewards/awards/bonuses, you can see a huge range of variances. Some people want time off work; the opportunity to bring a child to work for a day; lunch with the boss; a letter or certificate from the boss; rewards of small tokens such as flowers; tickets to events; gift certificates; the list can be endless. It is important to note that none of the above are very expensive, and some cost nothing. Being able to reward your people in ways that they individually value can bring the greatest rewards of all! Learning about how your employee wants to be acknowledged is part of the *PACT* process.

The Way-to-Go System of Acknowledgement
One effective method we have utilized successfully is the Way-to-Go system. It works like this: as the boss, you begin to create an environment where acknowledgement is an important ingredient of work life. You send emails, voicemails, make calls, or face-to-face individual acknowledgements of outstanding effort. You also encourage others to do the same for their peers. When you receive positive comments about one of your people, you share it with them as a "way-to-go." It's amazing how contagious this can be!

Make sure you include all three of the key components of acknowledgement: specificity, sincerity and timeliness.

One winning team we know gave each member ten "Way-to-Go" certificates to pass along to their teammates every time they caught them doing something to benefit the team. Since they worked together often, it was possible for everyone to be recognized for their contributions by their peers. Team members noted the particular accomplishment on the certificate, and when it was turned in, the boss saw and acknowledged the accomplishment as well.

You may also track these acknowledgements to employees with simple summary notes in a "way-to-go" file for that individual. You can also keep copies of acknowledgements they receive in that file. At some regular point in time, perhaps during a performance support meeting, you can sit with the employee and go through the file as a celebration of his great work. It is incredible how powerful and motivating this process can be! It also provides excellent data for completing formal reviews, if your organization requires them.

Feedback—the Other Side

Acknowledgement is a critical factor in great bossing. Together, acknowledgement and feedback make up an even bigger picture, one of *overall continuous performance improvement*. While feedback can and often is thought of as negative or critical, simply stated, we define feedback as the process of sharing your thoughts and opinions with someone regarding their performance in a constructive, supportive way. Now, although we can define it in simple terms, to actually practice providing feedback in the most effective and humane manner is truly an art. The *PACT*'ing boss becomes highly skilled and creative at the art of feedback.

Why Provide Feedback?

The purpose of providing feedback is principally twofold:

1. Feedback clarifies how the individual's performance is viewed by the boss and others, the value of the individual's contribution, what he is doing well and what he could be doing better.
2. Effective feedback provides tremendous development opportunities for continuous performance improvement, as each feedback session can become a coaching session, involving discussions on how the individual can continue to grow, enhance skills, job performance and attain goals.

Time and Place for Feedback

PREPARATION:

Before you begin to have a dialogue including feedback, take a few moments to collect your thoughts, explore your intentions and make a plan. Considering the following points is a great way to prepare for an informal feedback session:

- What is your intention behind providing this feedback?

  If it is *not* an intention related to truly supporting the positive and successful growth and development of the individual as well as the team/organization, we suggest rethinking your intentions and comments before proceeding.

- How can you provide the information in a way that is aligned with your supportive intention? In other words, how can you state your feedback in a constructive versus destructive way? (We will also speak more on this topic in Chapter 8—Trust.)

105

HOW OFTEN:

In the Acknowledgement section of this chapter, we spoke of the need for frequency. We believe the same is true for feedback; the rule is to provide *regular* feedback. We will discuss this in more detail in this chapter's section on *Performance Support*. For now, let's simply say that it is important to have a regularly scheduled time to sit one-on-one with your employees and have an informal dialogue concerning their progress. The frequency of these meetings can vary, depending on the nature of the work and the individual—anywhere from weekly to monthly typically works well. Additionally, don't forget that the acknowledgement piece of this process works best if it happens even more frequently.

WHERE:

A simple statement regarding the "where" of constructive feedback: never in public. It is difficult enough for some people to receive constructive feedback; it is almost always destructive—certainly not supportive and nurturing—to comment on someone's needs for improvement in front of colleagues or other associates. Find a quiet, private place where the employee will feel safe and comfortable. If this is in a private office, it is best if you can avoid sitting behind a desk, as this can be very intimidating. Pull a chair around to the front or side of the desk, so that the barrier of the impersonal desk is not between you. Also, avoid sitting too close and invading the individual's personal space.

A word of caution about the limitations of providing constructive feedback in email or other methods of written communication. Writing only provides a one-way information stream and can seem threateningly formal if it involves criticism. There is no way to check out how your information is being received, nor is there any expedient way for the receiver to clarify issues, ask questions, or check out what they might be "making up" about what you are saying. The opportunity to have a true face-to-face, or at least voice-to-voice dialogue is definitely better than in writing. We suggest limiting the use of written feedback to following up a previous feedback conversation, or as an additional piece of information included in a face-to-face or voice-to-voice dialogue. Certainly in the case where liability and risk issues are of concern, having such back-up documentation may be advisable. And certainly in such high-risk situations, it is critical to review such written documentation, as well as plans for the dialogue with HR or legal counsel in advance. Of course providing a fully positive acknowledgement is OK to do in writing sometimes. However, we would even suggest here to use a combination of verbal and written—don't hide behind the keyboard/pen!

It's a lot to think about, we know. And, it gets easier with more practice—we promise!

Putting Acknowledgement and Feedback to Work Through the Performance Support Process

We introduced the term: *Performance Support* in Chapter 3. We believe this term is much more descriptive and conducive to the successful process of helping people do the best job they can possibly do and helping the company to better manage its human capital than the traditional *Performance Management* process. The term Performance Management falls much more into the old ways of command and control style management, as opposed to humane leadership. Indeed, what produces more sweaty palms on both sides of the desk than the traditional once a year performance review?

True leadership is all about supporting performance: supporting people in such a way so they have the tools, resources, training, and ongoing guidance and mentorship needed to do the best job they possibly can. This sets up the best success scenario for the organization and the individual. And, one of the most effective tools for doing this is The People*PACT Performance Support* Process. In other words, this is where you create and sustain the *PACT*, along with annual performance goals.

This process includes:
1. Setting goals, objectives and action plans in alignment with the organization's mission and strategies. It also includes setting personal professional goals, then identifying specific ways the leader can support the employee's efforts to accomplishing goals and successfully fulfill the expectations of the job. This is the *PACT*.
2. Setting regular sessions, monthly (at a minimum), for one-on-one time, approximately 30 minutes to 1 hour, in informal discussion.

The purpose of these sessions is twofold:
   a. They provide regular opportunities to clarify roles/goals/expectations and check in on the status of accomplishment.
   b. They offer a tremendous opportunity for the leader to provide support/mentoring/encouragement and problem-solving through ongoing supportive

conversation. Including these topics in ongoing meetings avoids any "surprises" down the road, and most importantly, helps to ensure commitment to and execution of the *PACT*.

A real *Performance Support* session is not like a traditional "review." It is an opportunity to acknowledge your people for what they have done well, clarify the areas in which they have learned and developed, and to dialogue with them about how they can augment their skills to perform even better in the future and come closer to achieving their goals. For a *PACT* boss, a support session is also an opportunity to recommit to the *PACT*, redefine each other's business objectives, and review what you need from the employee to fulfill the team's goals. It is about discovering what, specifically, the employee feels will enable her to do her job more effectively in the future. The *PACT* boss will spend time discussing big picture objectives, then zeroing in on what the employee hopes to gain from her efforts, whether it is future advancement, further development, increased pay, an enhanced benefits package or other personal benefits.

The actual conversation could include any one or more of the following topics:

a. Review of the individual's progress on annual goals, objectives, projects, and the *PACT*.
b. Discuss any issues that may have arisen during the month, where the leader could serve as a coach and provide developmental support for the employee.
c. Take this time to get to know the employee better. This is when you can learn about what is truly

important to her, and what motivates her to give the most at work. How does she like to be acknowledged? Learning more about her outside interests, family, hobbies, etc., can also help to build a greater level of trust and an environment of support and collaboration.

d. Discuss any behaviors and/or individual activities that might be impacting work outcomes.

e. Include constructive comments around areas that need improvement.

f. Provide the full perspective by tying the individual's goals into the team and organizational goals.

g. Reinforce your end of the bargain during these conversations. This feedback is a crucial component in the process of fulfilling the *PACT*.

h. Remember that acknowledgement, when applied appropriately, can be the most effective single component of the feedback process, as building on our strengths is the foundation of high performance, according to Buckingham and Clifton (2001). They assert that what makes organizations great is capitalizing on individuals' strengths, as well as viewing differences across employees as opportunities. Always try to end your session with a specific, sincere acknowledgement.

Finally, be sure to turn on your "self awareness" antenna now, too. Not only do you want to take time to consider the language you will use—constructive versus critical—you also want to be aware of your body language and your intonation. Feedback sessions are a great opportunity for growth, and yet they are a delicate situation for egos as well. Please tread carefully down this road.

ACKNOWLEDGEMENT & FEEDBACK

If you are required to provide an annual evaluation, you can pull together the highlights of your monthly meetings to provide the employee with a yearly performance review. If you are like most *PACT* bosses, you will find that, by following the process we recommend, annual reviews become more productive than ever—AND easier! This process helps avert the dreaded situation where the annual review contains "surprising" information, since the *Performance Support* has been a regular conversation over the course of the entire year. This process also helps avoid the common annual review problem that the focus is typically only on the last three months of the past year. And don't forget to draw from the "Way-to-Go" file for review and celebration of each employee's major accomplishments! When you list all the ways the employee has succeeded over the review period and give examples that show you really took notice, the employee can feel the support. They feel capable and appreciated and from that place can more comfortably look for ways to grow and improve. Performance reviews can cease being dreaded for both employees and managers and can become celebrations of success and growth.

Let's take a look at some sound bites from a *Performance Support* session Diane had with Rick.

Diane was happy to see Rick as it had been several weeks since they had been in the office at the same time due to their horrendous travel schedules.

Diane began by asking "So Rick, how was celebrating your daughter's birthday on the beach in Florida?"

After a couple minutes of personal catching up, Diane said, "When we met last month, we agreed to focus some of our conversation today on the Customer

Service Initiative, since your project around the new point-of-service customer survey was just getting underway. So, how are things going thus far?"

Rick began, "Things went great with getting them out to all the health centers. Administrators were more than happy to put them in the patient information brochure racks. What I'm worried about, is that we have only received five back for the entire month, and the centers had 22,000 outpatient visits. I'm worried about not getting a significant response rate."

"Well, it's great news that the administrators were supportive. They have a lot of pressure on them to demonstrate a high level of service, and this is the tool they have been waiting for. Have you thought about attending their monthly meeting to brainstorm about ways to increase response rates?" Diane further offered, "Part of our PACT is for me to find opportunities for you to interact with the clinical side of the house, and this seems like a perfect place to do so. I'll make sure Calvin supports the effort by getting you on their meeting agenda."

Diane continued, "Do you think this meeting with the administrators might be a good opportunity to practice some of the Appreciative Inquiry skills you picked up at your workshop?"

"Absolutely" replied Rick. "I know in the past I have used my problem-solving and 'hard sell' tactics with this group—and as we both know—they often backfired. So, this time I think I can be much more effective with this new approach."

"I'd be willing to work with you on practicing a little before the meeting if you'd like..." Diane offered.

"That would be great because I'm sure I'll be a little nervous" Rick replied. "Thanks so much!"

They talked further about how Rick's old hard sell tactics did not work well in the organizational culture at Health Assurance. Rick also promised to update Diane during their meeting next month, if not sooner, on how the administrators meeting went.

In closing, Diane concluded by complimenting Rick, "You know Rick, it is great to see how quickly and effectively you have incorporated the Appreciate Inquiry skills into the way you present and influence. Your questions come across sincere and supportive, and I have watched folks respond very positively to you. You are already making a significant impact on turning things around in your department and keeping people happy in the process. This is really awesome to see!"

Now, go back and see how many of components *a* through *h* above that Diane incorporated into this conversation, AND in only a few minutes! By-the-way, Rick had a great session with the administrators and they came up with a workable solution that immediately proved successful: receptionists passed out a survey with a pen to each patient upon check in, with a personal request to please complete it. Response rates then continued to exceed the goal!

How Much Extra Effort is this — and is it Worth it?

You may be wondering, "But how much of my time is this going to consume? How can I fit this in on top of all the fires I have to put out, and my never-ending 'To Do' list?" We contend that the extra 30 to 40 minutes per team member per month, plus the extra one or two minutes of acknowledgement a week, will actually free up time, particularly in those fire-fighting efforts. Imagine if in our previous story Rick and Diane had not begun working on a solution to the poor response rate early in the process. It could have been months before it was detected and solved, thus leaving a huge "incomplete" goal on demonstrating levels of customer service for the entire region!

How many of your fires could have been avoided if employees were more clear on what they needed to do—if you were more clear on what was expected of them and how it was going—before it had already gone down the tube? If, for example, an employee whose goal is advancement has been assigned to a specific project, you might reaffirm the *PACT* and review his progress by asking, "How are you doing with those three goals we discussed?" His answer will let you know whether he is meeting his goals—and yours. Remind the employee of the steps he has agreed to take to complete his part of the *PACT* and discuss what can be done to head off problems or make his work easier. Then, talk about your piece of the *PACT*, allowing for reflection on your end as well. The *PACT* has again been acknowledged and reinforced; the session is complete. This is what those ongoing update conversations can provide, thus helping to alleviate more complicated problems down the road. Even with those difficult conversations, this approach pays off. As Susan Scott (2002, p.23) writes in her book, *Fierce Conversations*, "Fierce conversations often do take time. The problem is, anything else takes longer."

Ongoing Maintenance of the *PACT*

Be sure that you are not using these sessions to micromanage; if the conversation is taking too much time, you might consider your level of involvement in small details.

Renegotiate the *PACT* promptly when circumstances change. Mergers happen; company and governmental policy shifts; markets and customers change. A sudden change in company policy may result in the loss of some of your bargaining chips. For example, if the organization is no longer paying the continuing education fees of certain employees and a member of your team has been counting on that reward, don't let the *PACT* fall apart. Explain that the change is beyond your control, but that you intend to support the employee nevertheless. Then search for an alternative. You might promise to stick your neck out with the powers that be and try to "grandfather" the employee in despite the recent changes. Or you might agree on a new goal, such as time-off, a bonus, important commendation or an exciting project. The beauty of the *PACT* is that it is a fluid process. Flex it to conform to the times, and your team will feel supported no matter what the business climate.

Following this method of ongoing feedback and *Performance Support* will bring benefits that you may only dream of now. Your employees will be clear on their roles and responsibilities; they will consistently know where they stand relative to performance, and, most importantly, they will feel that they have a boss who is there to support them in attaining their goals. This leads to highly satisfied, highly productive employees. And we all know the impact this can have on the bottom line of an organization!

So as we have seen here, acknowledgement and its other half, feedback, make up the larger picture of continuous performance improvement. Delivered regularly in a systematic *Performance Support Process*, with humane leadership principles, including a *PACT*, you and your employees can work miracles in your organization. You can truly accomplish the breakthrough results—personally and professionally—that you both desire.

Chapter 7
COLLABORATION

"Leadership has a harder job to do than just choose sides. It must bring sides together."

— *Jesse Jackson*

Individuals Working Together Bring Exponential Benefits

Collaboration is the art of working effectively with others. Collaboration—doing it and helping others learn to do it—is one of the most important skills a boss can develop on the road to becoming a truly great leader. Employees are more motivated to achieve if they feel ownership of the business or project. People want to be included and consulted in their workplace. They want to contribute. When they get a chance to participate, share ideas and learn new skills they are grateful and want to "give back" to the team, the boss, or the company.

Key Ingredients for Collaboration

Creating an environment where effective collaboration is the norm for all interactions requires a number of key ingredients. Understanding, perspective and trust are important elements for collaboration. Since these are all elements of the *PACT*, can you see how making the *PACT* can pay off through greater collaboration, greater synergies?

Since bringing the big picture perspective is one of the first steps on the road to collaboration, let's quickly review how this works. To better gain the full picture perspective, it is important to have a reasonable level of understanding of others involved. This includes understanding their goals, their perspectives and opinions on the issue, and their experiences. This knowledge enhances understanding of all the elements involved in the issue, which in turn enhances the breadth and depth of the picture of understanding that is being painted. Sometimes people look and sound as though they are in agreement on the surface while a deeper understanding of their needs and issues can reveal that over time they will diverge in direction and goals. This can be avoided by spending the time early on to explore people's core motivations and find ways to blend, combine or negotiate outcomes and approaches. This greater depth of understanding helps bring people together, which is critical for effective collaboration. We covered this in the Chapter 5—Perspective, therefore, we will direct our attention on additional elements in this chapter.

In this chapter, we will focus on the following key elements we believe are also essential skills for leaders who want to be successful in collaboration and *PACT*'ing:

- Ability to bring people into alignment;

- Understanding of the process to create and sustain high performing teams;
- Ability to work through conflict, or as we prefer to call it—"conflict transformation."

Let's take a look at each of these elements, but first, here's a story about the art of effective collaboration.

Diane hired two new sales associates six months ago, each from two different competing health plans. Roger and Pat had both come from companies with cultures that were very competitive; all sales goals were on individual performance and each worked on a compensation plan where percent of sales was a significant component of their pay. Diane had thought that the strategy and tactics of Health Assurance, which focused on team effort and performance, would be a welcome change for Roger and Pat.

To her surprise, she found that over the first four months of their employment, Roger and Pat were not connecting with the rest of the sales team, and even worse, they were constantly firing zingers at each other, often times veiled in humor, but with clear undercurrents of competition and criticism. As fate would have it, both Roger and Pat's key accounts announced a corporate merger, which, at first, had each of them fearing for their job. You see, at each of their former employers, when such mergers occurred, the "stronger" sales associate would "win" the new merged account and the other associate would "lose"—and often times, that meant losing their job.

*Diane knew there was enough business and po-
tential new business here to justify keeping both
of them on board and decided to capitalize on this
opportunity to help shift Roger and Pat's personal
competitive paradigms into the Health Alliance collaborative culture. She brought them into her office individually and explained that she was going to set them
up as "co-account managers" for the new merged account. She let them talk about their initial reactions,
including distrust, anger, confusion and fear. She had
developed a strong enough relationship with each of
them that they were open with her. She explained her
concerns about their resistance to shifting into a more
collaborative mode. To her surprise, they each independently told her they envied the other sales associates and how they supported each other. It was just
hard for them to make that shift with each other since
they had come from competing plans and often lost
accounts to each other in the past. They also admitted that despite their frequent barbs, they actually saw
strengths in the other. Diane had found her common
thread! She then brought them together to begin setting the foundation of the partnership account management arrangement.*

*Roger and Pat each identified what they saw as
the strengths and value they brought to the partnership, and also noted where they had weaknesses.
They talked about how they could capitalize on those
strengths and help support the weaknesses. They collaboratively identified and agreed upon the goals and
performance outcome measures and clearly defined
each of their roles and responsibilities. Furthermore,*

they talked about how working cooperatively could help them achieve the goals, and they discussed how they would work together and communicate. Diane also set them up with an executive coach who worked with partner leaders and would support them through building the relationship.

Within three months, the turn-around in both Pat and Roger's attitudes and demeanors was phenomenal. They were well on their way to setting the groundwork of a collaborative relationship, and also interacting much more constructively with the other sales associates on the team, asking for their input on various issues. Six months into the partnership, Diane received a call from the customer, singing the praises of both Roger and Pat, and the value the team account management approach had brought to them as a client. They were now looking at a three-year contract! Diane was elated, as was the entire sales team, who would benefit from this "win," as their performance bonuses were not individual-based, but team-based.

Alignment

To effectively work together, to collaborate, one first and foremost needs a reason to do so. A shared, compelling vision is vital to effective collaboration. When two or more people strongly share a common goal or vision, the compelling nature of that vision can provide them with the strength and courage to work through long and/or difficult times. It is also the strength and excitement of that vision that can spur creativity and solutions.

A great leader helps bring others into alignment with that vision. When employees understand the rationale behind a particular vision or strategy, they are much better equipped to find their own way to embrace it, as well as create solutions and tactics and solve problems to help reach the vision. Information and understanding are essential to this buy-in and ownership. The need for this shared vision holds true across the continuum of size or scope of project, from the vision of international organizations all the way to the vision or strategy of specific projects that require a collaborative effort. If you cannot convince others of the need for or value of a particular vision, strategy or project, you are going to be hard pressed to engage their full cooperation in working on it with you.

To build this level of alignment, leaders must be fully equipped to listen for understanding so they can find where obstacles to alignment may lie. If a leader simply operates in the "telling mode"—telling people what has to happen rather than asking for real input—alignment will be hard to come by. The power of the leadership position can certainly force people to go through the motions of contributing what is required of them, but it is highly unlikely that you will have people operating in the most innovative and effective mode if they haven't had an opportunity to understand and find a personal fit or alignment with the vision or project. The opportunity to have an extraordinary outcome will be greatly diminished. Great leaders know this and put in the personal effort up front to get this enlistment, as they know it will save tremendous time throughout the process. Great leaders know that when people are fully engaged in an effort, creativity and productivity abound!

The concept of alignment between *vision, tactics,* and *culture* applies to individuals, teams and organizations (see Exhibit 7.1):

- *Vision* encompasses the compelling vision and the high level key strategies/goals and desired outcomes for success.
- *Tactics* define the specific actions required to achieve the vision and goals.
- Organizational *culture* is the environment in which people operate; it is the official and unofficial "way we do things" and "the way we treat each other." Essentially, it is the personality of the organization, comprised of the values, assumptions, norms and beliefs of the collective organization and is manifested in its behaviors. This is particularly seen in the behavior of leadership and in both official policies and practices, as well as unofficial behaviors and practices.

For an organization to be truly effective there must be strong alignment between the vision, tactics and culture. All employees need to have a clear understanding of each of these components, the value of aligning these components, AND how their individual work efforts contribute to this bigger picture.

The model of the *Concentric Circles of Organizational Excellence* illustrates how the organizational culture must be in alignment with vision/strategies and tactics to assure optimizing the achievement of execution of those strategies and tactics, and ultimately long-term sustainability and success. Making the *PACT* is one of the ultimate tools to creating and enhancing this alignment.

Concentric Circles of Organizational Excellence

A key element to ensuring quality and success and excellence lies in aligning your strategy and tactics with your organizational culture.

- Vision without Tactics provides great ideas, but no clear roadmap to achieve them.

- Tactics without Vision keeps activity level up, but with no clear focus or direction. Little is truly achieved.

- Alignment is critical between Vision and Tactics.

- The Organizational Culture must be in alignment with Vision and Tactics to assure optimizing the achievement of execution of the Vision and Tactics,and ultimately long term sustainability, success and excellence.

Exhibit 7.1

Creating and Sustaining
High Performing Teams

In a fairly unusual move, Calvin asked Diane to serve as the senior manager responsible for the newly restructured pharmacy services. Previously, these services had been subcontracted and operated independently of one another. Calvin had seen the value of a collaborative effort across pharmacy services while he was in the Northwest Region and knew that Diane would be the best of his senior leaders to support that happening here.

With Calvin's coaching, here is how Diane and her new pharmacy team made a huge impact on the bottom line. While running as "silo's", independent contract pharmacies, most of the eight operations were barely breaking even. Additionally, they did not communicate with or offer support for each other. Diane's first job was to work with the pharmacy managers to develop a vision of collaborative pharmacy services that resonated with each manager. Since they were all quality and service oriented, it was easy to take the Region's vision of quality of care and service and align it to a similar Pharmacy vision shared by all eight managers and sites. Next, the management group began to identify key goals that they all could support to enhance quality. As they further developed these goals, Diane gently helped them create tactics that required a collective, collaborative effort. Furthermore, the expected outcome of such efforts would far exceed any previous performances of any of the individual pharmacy sites. The goals were a stretch, but not

*unattainable. The group quickly realized the impor-
tance of sharing information and experiences—both
successes and others that did not work as expected.
They also began to appreciate the value of their bi-
monthly meetings where such information was shared,
including consistent review of the plan.*

*Best practices began to evolve. Through individu-
al coaching, Diane helped each of them realize their
personal fit and contribution to the effort. Trust was
building among the group, and they were beginning
to form a true team. By the end of the first twelve
months of internal collaborative operations, productivity had increased across all eight areas by an average of 18%. Expenses were down by 5% and revenues,
thanks to the new joint OTC sales project, were up
$1 million—a 72% increase. And Diane and the phar-
macy leadership team were most proud to see employee satisfaction increased by 58% and employee turnover decreased by 65%.*

*Do you think such success could have come with-
out the collaboration this team exhibited? The leadership team certainly believed that was the key, and
gladly shared the first bonus any of them had ever received across the team of eight managers as well as
their staffs.*

When a goal, project or task requires a high degree of cooperation and interdependence, then the need for an effective team process is critical. Such synergy can create levels
of innovation, creativity and accomplishment far greater
than any single individual could ever achieve alone.

An effective team capitalizes on the strength of each of its members. The team leader must first believe in this *synergy factor,* meaning that, on teams, 1 + 1 is much greater than 2.

Next, the leader needs to understand the basic components of high performing teams. There are many team models out there, most of them different take-offs from the original *form, storm, norm, perform* approach. One such model that deserves attention is the Drexler/Sibbet Team Performance Model (Drexler, Sibbet, Forrester, 1992), which offers seven steps to high performing teams (see Exhibit 7.2.):

- Orientation (Why am I here?)
- Trust Building (Who are you?)
- Goal/Role Clarification (What are we doing?)
- Commitment (How will we do it?)
- Implementation (Who does what, when, where?)
- High Performance (Wow!)
- Renewal (Why continue?)

So what is the bottom-line to leading great teams? We believe it is twofold:

(1) understanding the value of and the process for creating teams, and

(2) continuing to pay unending attention to the people-needs throughout the process. If the people aren't collaborating as effectively as possible, the team cannot be the best it could be. When people feel they have a contribution to make and an opportunity to make it in a respected and

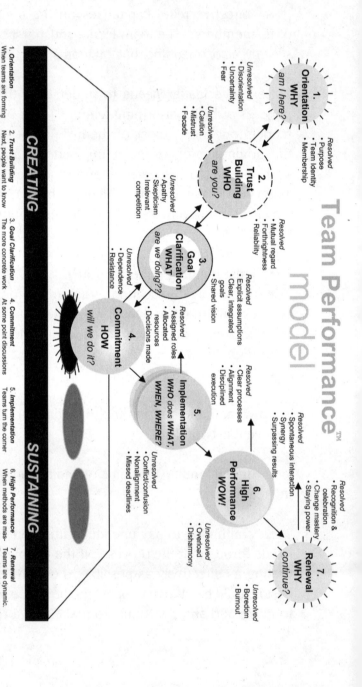

Team Performance™ model

1. Orientation
WHY
am I here?

Resolved
· Purpose
· Team Identity
· Membership

Unresolved
· Disorientation
· Uncertainty
· Fear

2. Trust Building
WHO
are you?

Resolved
· Mutual regard
· Forthrightness
· Reliability

Unresolved
· Caution
· Mistrust
· Facade

3. Goal Clarification
WHAT
are we doing??

Resolved
· Explicit assumptions
· Clear, integrated goals
· Shared vision

Unresolved
· Apathy
· Skepticism
· Irrelevant competition

4. Commitment
HOW
will we do it?

Resolved
· Assigned roles
· Allocated resources
· Decisions made

Unresolved
· Dependence
· Resistance

5. Implementation
WHO does WHAT, WHEN, WHERE?

Resolved
· Clear processes
· Alignment
· Disciplined execution

Unresolved
· Conflict/confusion
· Nonalignment
· Missed deadlines

6. High Performance
WOW!

Resolved
· Spontaneous interaction
· Synergy
· Surpassing results

Unresolved
· Overload
· Disharmony

7. Renewal
WHY
continue?

Resolved
· Recognition & celebration
· Change mastery
· Staying power

Unresolved
· Boredom
· Burnout

CREATING

1. Orientation
When teams are forming everybody wonders WHY they are here, what their potential fit is and whether others will accept them. People need some kind of answer to continue.

2. Trust Building
Next, people want to know WHO they will work with — their expectations, agendas and competencies. Sharing builds trust and a free exchange among team members.

3. Goal Clarification
The more concrete work of the team begins with need to end and decisions clarify about team goals, basic assumptions and vision. Terms and definitions come to the fore. WHAT are the priorities?

4. Commitment
At some point discussions must be made about HOW resources, time, staff—all will be managed. Agreed roles are key.

SUSTAINING

5. Implementation
Teams turn the corner when they begin to sequence work and settle on WHO does WHAT, WHEN, and WHERE in action. Timing and scheduling dominate this stage.

6. High Performance
When methods are mastered, a team can begin to change its goals and flexibly respond to the environment. The team can say, "WOW!" and surpass expectations.

7. Renewal
Teams are dynamic. People get tired, members change. People wonder "WHY continue?" It's time to harvest learning and prepare for a new cycle of action.

9.0 TPModel © 1999 Allan Drexler & David Sibbet

appreciated way, and when they understand the value of the collective effort to achieve a common purpose, nothing short of miracles can happen!

Conflict Transformation

Disagreements and conflict are an entirely normal part of any process in the work place. One can never totally avoid it, nor would one want to, as disagreements often spring from the diversity of thinking and opinion which you need in a thriving workplace. However, there can also be those conflicts that arise when someone believes her opinion is *the* opinion, and doesn't hold the space to consider other ideas. This is where the rub can come, and can often get in the way of moving forward effectively. There are many things a leader can do to decrease the quantity, as well as the intensity and duration, of conflict. In many cases, the outcome of successfully working through conflict can be extraordinary and lead to what we have seen to be true transformation of relationships, processes and systems

Leaders often avoid dealing with conflict, hoping it will go away or resolve itself. Sometimes that happens, but more often, the disagreement and conflict grows deeper, whether overtly or covertly, and continues to get in the way of how effectively people work together. It can lead to withholding information, distrust, confusion around vision/roles/goals, hidden agendas, time lost in petty bickering or gossiping, rumors, complaining, lying...the list can go on for a couple more chapters! You get the picture—you've certainly seen this happen in your own work experience. Does the humane leader allow disagreements and conflict to go down such counter-productive roads? Absolutely not! The humane leader is concerned about her people, their level of job satisfaction as well as productivity, and does not let conflict go too far. The great leader faces it head on, in a very humane way. We have discovered a relatively simple process that can be tremendously helpful to leaders in facilitating working through conflict. It is summarized below in four steps (see Exhibit 7.3.). Conflict work is one of the great opportunities where leaders can pull together all their humane skills and truly help lead to tremendous outcomes.

We offer the following model, which follows the People*PACT* Process and Principles of Humane Leadership as a guide for working through disagreements and conflict.

This process can:

- Help clear your thinking;
- Help clear thinking between you and your colleague;
- Help practice accountability;
- Help keep you behaving authentically;
- Enhance problem solving;
- Bring transformation in behavior, relationship patterns and in performance.

People*PACT* —
Conflict Transformation Model

We don't know many people who love to engage in difficult conversations around conflict. This is not something to approach lightly. As a matter of fact, we have found that a little preparation work pays off tremendously. Preparation helps you think through all the key steps of the conversation, as well as check out your own "issues" around the issue. Once you have prepared, you can more readily open up the conversation and seek solution. And finally, it is critical that you follow up on your part of the commitment for the solution.

We believe most individual conflicts can be worked through with effective dialogue. It may take more than one conversation. However, we have found many times that a single, well planned dialogue can do the trick! Whether it takes one or several, it all happens one conversation at a time.

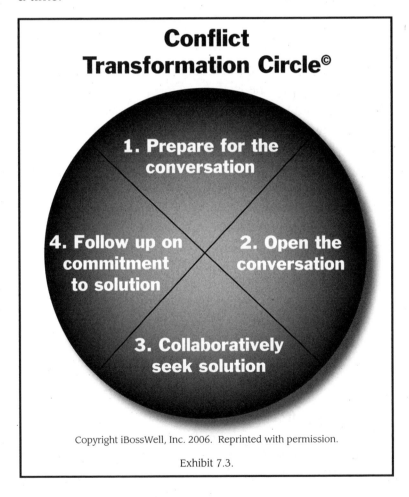

Conflict Transformation Circle©

1. Prepare for the conversation

2. Open the conversation

3. Collaboratively seek solution

4. Follow up on commitment to solution

Copyright iBossWell, Inc. 2006. Reprinted with permission.

Exhibit 7.3.

Conflict Transformation Circle©
Model Summary

I. Prepare for the conversation
1. Check your intention
2. Plan how you will Open the Door for Dialogue

II. Open the conversation
1. Open the Door
2. Share your intention
3. Share your contribution to the issue
4. Describe the issue
5. Align issue with vision and what is at risk
6. State your desire to find solution and resolve collaboratively

III. Collaboratively seek solution
1. Invite response—listen for understanding
2. Brainstorm for solution
3. Close conversation with confirmation of agreed upon solution and plan

IV. Follow-through on your commitment to solution
1. Do what you said you would do
2. Follow up with partner
3. Acknowledge efforts and successes

See Appendix B for a worksheet and example that you can use to help you prepare for these conflict transformation conversations.

Steps to Conflict Transformation

I. Prepare for the conversation

1. Check your intention:

   - Is your intention trustworthy?
     In other words, it is to truly find an answer to the issue and a solution to the situation that meets both of your needs, as well as addresses the underlying causes.

   - Be clear on the higher order vision or purpose that overarches the issue/problem and check if your intention behind having this conversation is in alignment with that vision/purpose. The higher order purpose here could simply be your desire to have a positive working relationship with your colleague. Check to make sure it is not driven by a personal preference or underlying agenda that is not in alignment with the vision or team values.

2. Preparing to Open the Door for Dialogue:

   - Consider how can you say what you want to say without blame, judgment, attack or defense.

   - How you start/open the dialogue can make or break your chances for a positive outcome. If you start out with blame, judgment, attack or defense more than likely the other person will put up a wall of "defense"—or get on the "offense." Either way, it sets up an instant barrier to open, constructive dialogue, listening, understanding and problem solving. And, you can actually cause more problems with a poor opener.

   - An effective way to do this is to state your opening in such a way that you hold the other person "safe" and leave yourself open/vulnerable.

3. Recognize your contribution to the issue/problem:
   - This is your opportunity to help keep the other person safe by you opening yourself up to vulnerability by acknowledging your part of the problem... "I dropped the ball by not telling you about..." or "I have been holding this in and have added to the problem by not seeking solution earlier..."

4. Outline the issue objectively—with a specific example:
   - Remember state the "objective data": "I observed...I saw...I heard..."
   - It is important to not include what you have "made up" in this step...rather, just the facts.

5. Identify what is at stake, relative to the vision.

6. Think about possible solutions—without getting stuck on your ideas here.

II. Open the Conversation

1. Open the Door;
2. Share your intention for the conversation;
3. Share your contribution to the issue/problem;
4. Describe the issue (just the facts/objective data);
5. Describe how you see this impacts the vision and what is at risk:
   - Here you can reinforce your intention to align with the big picture/compelling vision and your authentic desire for resolution.
6. State your desire to collaboratively find solution and willingness to work together to resolve the issue.

III. Collaboratively seek solution

1. Invite input/thoughts/reaction:
   - "I would like to hear your thoughts on this..."
   - Listen for understanding, not to convince or convert. This is not a debate.
   - After they have expressed their thoughts, check out your assumptions or what you are "making up" for further clarification of understanding.
2. Brainstorm possible solutions:
   - It's ok to make your constructive request here and discuss the feasibility.
3. Confirm the agreement, solution, and or summary to close:
   - Clarify the agreement to the solution and/or next steps.
   - Restate your commitment to follow through on your part of the solution.
   - Acknowledge & thank your partner.

IV. Follow-through on your commitment to solution

1. Do what you said you would do. The only thing worse that a poor opener is coming to agreement, then not following through on your commitment.
2. Check in with your partner to see how things are going.
3. Acknowledge your partner's efforts and success. Be supportive.

Often times this process is all you need to resolve many issues. Sometimes, if the same issue has repeatedly come up, it may be helpful to explore the deeper underlying causes.   Most times well-intended colleagues/partners with pure intentions can potentially work through this on their own, and there may be times when the support and facilitation of a coach/counselor is helpful.

This process allows an opportunity to create, redefine or expand the *PACT* with the other person, using **P**erspective to take into account the big picture, **A**cknowledgement to show that each person recognizes the value of the other, **C**ollaboration to ensure that everyone is represented in the solution and **T**rust to build a *PACT* that has enduring meaning and will be carried out with confidence.

Please remember:
- Ensure your intention is aligned with your compelling vision (not based in fear).
- Listen for understanding.
- Keep the compelling vision at the forefront.
- Remember to state your concerns without blame, judgment, attack or defense. And do this by saying it in such a way that you keep the other person safe and leave yourself vulnerable.
- Please end with acknowledgement and a "thank you".

Here's a story that clearly illustrates the value of this process.

Bridgette was the leader for a marketing develop-ment team in Diane's department. Her team was given the challenge of creating a proposal for a new customer, BigGuy Foods, who would be, if landed, the firm's largest customer to date. This customer was cur-rently a client of Health Assurance's largest competitor.

This was a great opportunity for both the company and Bridgette's team; she was excited, honored and nervous. One of the first steps in the action plan her team developed for this project was to gather market data. Bridgette depended on Ted's market research team for this information. She had included Ted and his senior researcher in the planning process, knowing their input was extremely valuable and critical to the success of this project. One week into the project, Ted was missing his deadlines and responding to Bridgette's emails and calls with only cryptic notes of "We'll get to it as soon as we complete our own urgent project."

Bridgette became increasingly frustrated, as her team was approaching the deadline for submission of the Request for Proposal (RFP) response and needed Ted's research information to proceed. She requested a meeting with Ted to discuss the situation. She had observed Diane in the past exhibit great skills in approaching difficult conversations, so Bridgette decided this would be a good opportunity to practice some of those techniques. The day before the meeting, she spent about 15 minutes planning for this conversation.

When she met with Ted, Bridget opened with, "Thanks so much for meeting with me, Ted. I heard about the big project that just got put on your plate and imagine you must be swamped right now." Ted nodded his head in agreement, arms crossed over his chest. Bridgette continued, "I wanted to talk with you about the BigGuy's proposal. As you know, we are having some challenges in completing the proposal, and I really need your help. My intention in talking to you is to try to find a solution that works for all of us—your team, my team, and especially Health Assurance so we can land this account."

Ted seemed to loosen his grip around his chest a bit, which Bridgette read as a sign she could continue. "When we met and created the plan to develop this proposal, we agreed this was a top priority project and that we had to meet certain deadlines. The first deadline was having competitive data in by May 20. It is now June 15 and the data has not yet been submitted. Without that data, we cannot build the services package to offer BigGuy. I have been remiss in meeting the deadline too by not talking with you about this before today."

Bridgette then asked, "Would you agree that deadline has been missed?"

Ted nodded his head in agreement and said, "Yes, we really got caught up in this other project."

Bridgette then said, "Since we both agree this is a critical project, and both agree that the proposal needs to get in on time, let's talk about how we can get there. I want you to know that I am willing to have my team support you in any way we can to not only meet the BigGuy deadline, but also help you on your other project. After all, both of our teams will benefit from the bonus if we land this account! I'd really like to hear your ideas about how we can best move forward."

Ted's phone rang and he saw it was the company president. He asked Bridgette, "I need to take this call from Calvin; can I get back with you this afternoon so we can come to resolution on this, say 1:30?" Bridgette agreed and left Ted's office.

After his call, Ted began to think about how Bridgette really seemed sincere about wanting to work with him and support his efforts. This was a different Bridgette than the one he thought he knew. Her team had won the "Team of the Year" award last year, while Ted's team came in third. He really resented that, as he felt his team had worked just as hard as Bridgette's and had landed as much work for the company. He resented that Bridgette seemed so well liked by the boss and wrote her off as the boss's favorite. Ted felt that Bridgette was overly aggressive and only out for herself. His direct experience with her on this project, however, dispelled some of these assumptions. Bridgette had not been aggressive at all, quite the contrary; she had been incredibly understanding and supportive, and he had also seen that her team had the utmost respect for her. He was also impressed by how well she enlisted her team in decision-making and plan development. And finally, he appreciated how she came to him to discuss his lack of cooperation with this project in a very supportive way, instead of a judgmental and blaming way. "Wow," he thought to himself, "Bridgette is not at all what I thought she was like.

At 1:30, Bridgette came back to Ted's office, and this time he started, "Bridgette, I'm really sorry I haven't met the deadlines. I've figured out how I can get caught up and get you all the information you need by the day after tomorrow. Then, if you'd like, I can help you through the analysis so that you can still meet your deadline. Would that work for you?"

Bridgette was shocked and delighted. "Absolutely! That will work great for us. And what about your other project? Can we help with that?"

"No, thanks. I actually think we're in pretty good shape with that project now. So let's focus on BigGuy to get that done!" Ted responded.

They went on to work out the details for completing the proposal. The proposal was completed a day ahead of schedule, and Health Assurance landed the BigGuy Foods account.

So, what did we see happen here? First, Ted had a negative impression of Bridgette and resisted supporting her and her team. Bridgette approached Ted in a non-threatening, non-blaming, supportive way, and worked through the conflict in a direct yet positive way. Given some time to reflect, Ted realized he had a misimpression of Bridgette (look what he had "made up"), and she really wasn't so bad after all. She also helped him realize the significance of their project (*perspective*), and even though he didn't want to admit to her what was holding him back from cooperating, he was totally committed to moving forward and working productively with her in the future.

Ted and Bridgette's story is a great example of the incredible outcomes that can be realized by working through conflict and having true collaboration.

We now encourage you to see what opportunities you can maximize through effective collaboration and teaming. How can you effect positive change for the individuals you work with, your organization and perhaps yourself, too? As a team leader and/or a *PACT*'ing boss, there will inevitably be conflict here and there. How you handle it will not only impact the effectiveness of your efforts and success (or not), how you behave in conflicting situations will serve as a model for how your team will behave. Don't you want that to be as effective, efficient and pain-free as possible? Although we certainly did not provide a fully comprehensive narrative on transforming conflict to solution, we hope the suggestions and tools provided in this chapter will inspire you to go out and find that opportunity to truly accelerate achievement of extraordinary outcomes through effective collaboration!

Chapter 8
TRUST — BUILDING THE FOUNDATION

"Honesty is the cornerstone of all success, without which confidence and ability to perform shall cease to exist."

— *Mary Kay Ash*

Great Performance Grows Where Trust Abounds

Trust — What it Means in an Organization

To create a trusting environment where people feel safe enough to take risks, and where mistakes are considered experiments to be learned from, is the best way to prepare employees for greatness. Truth and trust are the foundations for safe, productive work environments: telling the truth without blame, judgment, attack or defense is the ultimate trust-builder. In this type of environment high growth prevails, and people are happy, satisfied and give their best each day on the job. A great boss learns how to create and sustain this kind of work environment.

What happens when there is not a culture of trust within an organization? Ron Zemke (2000, pp. 76-83) aptly described current research on organizational trust, particularly lack thereof, as follows:

> The organizational consequences of low trust are a culture of insecurity, high turnover, marginal loyalty and, often, damaged customer relations.... research on trust found compelling evidence that low levels of trust in a work force can indeed lead directly to high stress, reduced productivity, stifled innovation, slowed decision-making, and indirectly, to low morale, high turnover and frequent absenteeism.

Trust is not something you can build overnight. How does a conscientious leader create and sustain such an environment? Research shows several keys to success in this arena, as does the experience of many successful leaders. We believe the foundation is based on truth.

Truth-Telling: the Highest Road to Building Trust

Speaking the truth appropriately takes practice, conscientiousness, sensitivity and mindfulness. It also takes awareness to distinguish between what you consider to be truth (which is often your opinion), and truth as determined by the objective data.

Let's consider this for a minute. Many people get caught up in a self-righteous campaign to "tell the truth," regardless of the consequences or impact on those with whom they are being so truthful. However, in many cases, "the truth" is simply a personal opinion or interpretation presented as fact. One of the keys to humane leadership is to consider the impact your words and actions might have on others. Ask yourself, what is my intention in wanting to make this statement? Am I keeping his well-being, integrity and personal growth in mind? Am I keeping the compelling vision of the organization in mind? Or am I just thinking of myself, and what I want?

It is also critical to distinguish fact from opinion. What is the objective data? What would a video of the situation show, versus your or someone else's interpretation of the scene on the video? In a truth-telling conversation, it is typically good to begin by stating the objective data.

Of course, as you may recall from the Conflict Transformation Model in Chapter 7, you want to begin a difficult conversation with checking, then stating, your intention. Make sure that your intention is based on your desire to have a positive working relationship with your colleague. Then begin by stating your intention to your colleague.

Then, if it is important (for growth and development, or for problem solving) to state your opinion, make sure you frame it as "your opinion." Now comes the true high art of this process. The art is in how you state your opinion. The key is in telling your truth (opinion) WITHOUT blame, judgment, attack or defense. Think about this. If you are truly going for the humane leadership approach, which is all about someone's growth and development, there is no room for, and only obstacles built by using blame, judgment, attack or defense. This is truly a trust-building opportunity!

This sounds good in theory, but it's always more difficult to put these concepts into practice. How can you do it? Linda Brown, president of Wolf Creek Partners, a leading Change Management organization, contends that the best way to speak your truth is by saying it in such a way that "you keep the other person safe and leave yourself vulnerable." Think about this for a minute. What if every time you had something difficult to say to someone, you said it in such a way that they were kept emotionally protected while you opened up yourself? Imagine the difference in the remainder of the conversation, where there was a lack of closing up, defensiveness, fear or intimidation of the other person, so they could better hear and process what you were saying. This openness then allows the conversation to continue in a much more open, productive way, bringing new insight and facilitating problem-solving.

Think about past conversations, where you have been on the receiving end of someone else's "truth" and felt blamed, judged, or worse—attacked. How effectively were you able to continue with a truly productive conversation? Sure, maybe you and the other person struggled through it, but to what end? And, if you are the boss, chances are you may never know the full impact of such an approach since the employee would likely not let you know how she is truly feeling. Typically, hard feelings show up more indirectly in low productivity, low morale, and ultimately turnover.

So let's talk a little more about how one speaks his truth in such a way that it leaves the other person safe, and at the same time, shows the human side—the vulnerable side—of the speaker.

Every email Mike received from Jan, Mike's new boss, had an automated return confirmation request attached. Diane, Mike's former boss, had never done this, and he found it quite disconcerting. Mike hadn't talked to Jan about her intentions behind always checking out receipt of her emails, but he sure had made up a lot of possible reasons about why she might be doing it. Most of them revolved around him feeling that Jan didn't trust that he was getting to his emails in a timely fashion, and that she was documenting her communications to him to build a case if he didn't get his work done satisfactorily. He had discussed this with several other team members who had similar impressions of Jan's practice with her email communications.

After several months this situation upset Mike to the point where he was finding himself spending an inordinate amount of time covering his tail with extra cc's on all communications, plus wasting time ruminating with colleagues about why Jan was so distrusting. He finally decided to approach. Mike was nervous about this, since Jan was his new boss, and he still couldn't read her very well. He started the conversation, "Jan, I noticed that you routinely include an automatic delivery receipt on your emails. I've been worried that perhaps you had concerns over my promptness with reading emails, so I thought I should check that out with you. Are you concerned about my timeliness?"

Jan, explained that in her former job, the IT system was so unreliable that many emails were lost, so it had just become her habit to do this. She had no lack of trust and was quite surprised by the impact of her actions. She thanked Mike for his courage to bring this

the People*PACT*®

*to her attention and spent the next staff meeting talk-
ing about trust. (She also immediately stopped including confirmation requests to her emails!)*

Although this scenario has a happy ending, it is unfortunate that so much time and effort was expended on non-
productive, potentially destructive behavior, just because
of something as simple as confirmation receipts. However,
as you saw in Mike's story, things are not always simple.
Employees are often sensitive to any actions that can be
misconstrued as distrusting, and it is critical for bosses to
be sensitive to this issue. Again, the need for self-awareness on the part of leaders is evident. It is important to
carefully consider every action that you take, and the possible impact it may have. Additionally, Mike's story reinforces the need for regular communication to keep in touch
with what's really going on in the work environment, as
well as the importance of developing a safe environment
built on honesty and trust.

Trust Takes Courage

As we have seen in earlier chapters, mutual trust is the
foundation upon which the *PACT* process is built. First and
foremost, a *PACT* boss must support and trust that people
will be who they are, not who the boss might hope them to
be. Most of the trust violations we see in the course of our
work occur among people who let each other down not
because of their personal failures, but because they have
failed to meet some assumed standard or expectation. Often, coworkers don't even share their expectations with

148

each other; instead they assume that, given a certain situation, everybody would behave essentially the same way.

Needless to say, it is critically important to communicate about basic team, organization or personal values, especially when you're working with a new team member. The following story illustrates a time when trust was truly the right path to take.

> *Elise was a veteran saleswoman in a very challenging territory. She was one of the few people who could manage the difficult customers she called on and could produce solid growth results year after year. Elise had taken some time off at the beginning of the year to have her second baby and was just getting back into the swing of work when the finance department called her manager. One of the vendors Elise was dealing with had called to report that he believed Elise was cheating the company. Diane, Elise's manager, was floored. She had been working with Elise for more than eight years. Although Diane knew Elise could be demanding and somewhat outspoken, she had never known her to be dishonest. Diane's boss, Calvin, however, was not so confident. "She must have just gone over the edge, Diane," Calvin commented. "The evidence is overwhelming. We are sending our finance representative to interview her but you will have to let her go. We just can't harbor a thief in this company."*
>
> *Diane was heartsick. She called Elise into her office and asked about the situation. Although Elise was very surprised, she gave a complete account of what she had done that might have alarmed the vendor. According to Elise, she was trying to juggle budgets in*

order to get the most value for her customer. In so doing, she had changed some dates. She summed her story up with a plea. "Diane, you know me. I would never steal from the company or let you down." Diane was facing a real dilemma. Elise had admitted to falsifying documents, however, she did not steal from her employer.

Early the next morning, Diane called Calvin. She told him, "I have found out the details of the incident and Elise has violated some of our policies, but she is not a thief. I believe there should be consequences here, but not termination. How about if we put her on probation and withhold her bonus until we're sure she understands the seriousness of this incident?"

Calvin thought it over. After considerable conversation with the legal and HR departments and more discussion with Diane about Elise's track record, he was willing to keep her in her job. Elise went on to work productively for many more years and proved herself a valuable employee to the organization. Her manager had put herself on the line for her, and she had gone the distance in her support.

Diane and Elise's story illustrates the challenge of continuing to trust in the face of difficult circumstances. As most bosses know, it isn't easy to maintain balance while walking the fine line between commitment to employees and commitment to the organization. Of course, as we have said, the *PACT* is a three-way agreement. That means that when it is optimally enacted, the boss, the employee and the organization will all be using the same road map. But what if they don't?

Following the Same Road Map

Every driver knows how easy it is to get a ticket. All you really have to do is fail to read a sign that other drivers observe. So it is easy to see how trust is violated in business when we don't make sure that every member is following the same course to arrive at success.

In this book, we talk a lot about creating "alignment" at the team level. At the boss/employee level, a lack of alignment is often misinterpreted as a lack of cooperation, poor skills or a lack of respect, among other things. Over time, the lack of a shared focus will undermine even the most talented group of individuals. The actions and reactions that result from it can become very costly and damaging to both the boss and the employee. And, this void of alignment will always erode trust.

The story that follows is an all-too-common illustration of the way a collaborative environment breaks down when team members are not fully aligned and trusting.

Sam came to Health Assurance, Inc., from a very successful junior executive position at his former company. A highly-sought recruit, Sam seemed to have every possible qualification, including glowing recommendations, a background as a community leader and a very impressive award for outstanding community service. Diane had heard good things about him from a client, and encouraged her colleague Ira to hire him. There was no doubt in people's mind that Sam was just the person to take over a newly-created role at Health Assurance.

Sam's assignment was to manage the training of about 90 new employees hired to support the company's recent expansion. Ira assumed that Sam knew how to set up an orientation and map out the logistics for a training program for these new people. While Ira gave him lots of information on the specifics Sam was to deliver, he tried to also give Sam the "space" he needed to work his magic. Unfortunately, Ira didn't take the time to provide Sam with the bigger picture perspective, like how this project fit in with the overall company goals and direction. Ira granted Sam considerable latitude on the overall management of the project and, as Ira expected, Sam seemed to hit the ground running.

It didn't take Sam long to win the approval of other managers involved with the project. These other managers had their own plates overflowing, so they welcomed Sam's offer to take on most of the load himself. In fact, they were happy to delegate the training responsibilities to such a well thought-of newcomer.

The training program development was supposed to take eight weeks. For the first few weeks, things seemed to be moving along very well. Sam had conducted an initial meeting with the team and essentially took the load of the project on himself. Unfortunately, he failed to connect with the team members so they could all gain clear understanding of the scope of the project, action plan accountabilities, and additional other initial team-building processes. They had no sense of his goals and personal intentions around the project. Sam wanted to make a big impression on his new boss and colleagues by essentially completing the *project himself. Sam did not fully grasp, nor did Ira explain, the full scope of this project, its implications and key stakeholders.*

Sam began to fall behind, missing key deadlines for various parts of the program. Moreover, reports began to trickle in from other employees and managers saying that Sam had failed to include them in some of the more important meetings. Had Ira not been busy with another project, he would have noticed Sam was struggling. Although he touched base with Sam to reaffirm the importance of the missing reports and ill-planned meetings, he wanted to believe that Sam was still on the right track. However, Ira's trust in Sam was beginning to weaken.

About two weeks after the project ended, Ira began to see Sam's project with some clarity. Sam had taken the matter into his own hands and subjected the participants to unnecessary confusion. He had altered the program to suit his personal needs rather than those of the organization. He had also been a poor manager of the financial resources he had been given. Distressed, Ira wrote Sam a memo outlining what he believed Sam had done and the steps to remediation that needed to be taken. The communication was formal and came without warning. Sam reacted angrily and filed a formal grievance with the company.

Over the next year, it became clear that Sam had made many mistakes and misjudgments. He may, in fact, have not been suited for the role he was given. Sam eventually left the company after creating great stress and expense. Neither Sam nor Ira performed at their best that year, and Sam was not the only one to suffer: Ira, too, lost credibility.

What can we learn from the example above? Why did such a promising newcomer fail to perform up to expectations? Where did his manager go wrong?

First they did not effectively form the *PACT*. If Ira had taken the time to provide Sam with the "big picture perspective" some of the ugly aftermath would surely have been avoided. Most of all, Ira assumed that Sam shared the values and knowledge of standard operating procedures that defined Health Alliance. To him, such knowledge seemed obvious. Based upon that belief, he gave Sam too much freedom too soon. Sam felt abandoned by his manager and began to act unilaterally—and disastrously. He did not trust that Ira was supporting him and his best interests. The miscommunications did not end there. When Sam failed to act in accordance with company policies and procedures, Ira assumed that the newcomer had violated his trust. He fired off a disciplinary memo without warning or discussion. In a very real sense, it was Ira who violated Sam's trust. His lack of clear communication about his concerns caused Sam to fear for his very career. Surely they both learned a great deal from this unfortunate experience. After a year-long battle with human resources, Sam left the company. The truth is, the entire event may have been avoided if a clear *PACT* had been established early on, with clear expectations, agreement on mutual support, frequent communication and building of trust.

What Happens When There is a Lack of Trust?

Probably every one can tell stories about work experiences where lack of trust led to numerous problems, lost time and productivity, turnover, inordinate stress and even sickness.

Leonard L. Berry (1999, p. 124), professor of marketing at Texas A&M University and author of *Discovering the Soul of Service*, has looked closely at the customer consequences of low employee trust: "Trust-based relationships characterize the sustained success of every company we studied for the book," he says. "Trust is equally important in creating employee and partner relationships. Just as customers abandon companies they do not trust, so do employees."

Berry's view is shared by Dennis Reina (1999, p. 7), co-author of *Trust & Betrayal in the Workplace*. Says Reina,

"We've seen countless change efforts and projects fail because of a lack of trust in the people initiating the change. We have seen vice presidents undermine each other, managers hide their opinions, and employees sabotage projects because they did not trust each other..."

There is a common phenomenon that comes with change efforts, and it has a lot to do with trust. As we see it, with most change efforts, there is a small group at one end of the continuum who are the visionaries and change agents; with another small group at the opposite end of the continuum who are often times sabotaging the change; and the vast majority are in the middle, waiting to see who they can best trust. Interestingly, some of those folks at the sabotage end may have been change agents at a different time who lost their trust in the system. Often times this trust is lost because they felt they were not heard, or that their ideas were discounted. Re-building trust with such individuals may be worth some effort, as they could become a true positive change agent once again.

the People*PACT*®

Another very real example relating to trust and truth-telling is in the healthcare industry and the reporting of medical errors. There are very few situations requiring more truth telling and trust than in the delivery of medical care. To continue to enhance the quality of care provided, it is critical that practitioners identify and report errors in a thorough and timely manner. This can, in the most extreme cases, literally save lives, and in all cases, can lead to great lessons learned, ultimately advancing the quality of medical care. Health Assurance began a significant effort to increase the reporting of medical errors years back in the "Murray days" (remember Murray? He was the CEO who was later terminated for poor leadership practice). It is an interesting story with many of its own lessons around truth and trust.

> *Murray assigned Diane's predecessor, Ralph, the project of developing a medical errors reporting project. There was already a policy and procedure in place for reporting errors; however, it was not used to the extent leadership believed would reflect the actual level of errors. Ralph knew that he had to have the Medical Group at the helm of this project, or it would not fly, so he enlisted the Medical Director, Pat, to be his co-chair. All went well with the creation of the program, as the physicians as well as the ancillary health providers and administrators all truly embraced the compelling vision of the project of improved safety and quality care. One of the keys, if not the absolute most important component of an error reporting program, is the need for complete trust that errors will be treated as opportunities for growth and learning, and for new skills building and problem solving, rather than be used as a*

156

club on the individual making the error. If fear of punishment and reproach are the norm not many people are going to run to fill out the error forms.

The work group building the errors reporting program knew this concept well and attempted to pave the path for building a safe and trusting environment. They set up tracking systems to watch for patterns (both with individuals and issues) so that training and/ or problem resolution and quality assessments could be conducted. Of course there were stop-gaps developed for safety purposes to watch for patterns of errors with the same individual; however, all knew that this was much more the exception than the rule.

The first six months the program was in place, error reporting increased significantly. The team was confident that this was truly an increase in reporting vs. actual errors, as their quality outcomes measurements stayed constant during the same time period. It appeared that the leadership training they conducted and the culture of trust and support they tried to build around this project was working.

What those first six months of experience also brought was a significant amount of data on errors. The Quality Assurance and Training teams were using this data for setting focus and priorities for training and skill-building. Murray took the data and starting sending individual emails to the managers of the practitioners who were reported as the cause of the errors, suggesting that they "keep an eye on them, and consider termination if it ever happened again..." There were no "thank you's" for supporting the new program, no acknowledgement of the enhanced learnings and training efforts that were underway to decrease *the errors, just "the fall of Murray's club" on the heads of these managers.*

Word got out of Murray's emails and you can imagine what happened: within two months the reporting rate had fallen to half the level of reports even before the initiation of the new program. Ralph was devastated. This was his last straw with Murray. He took the job the headhunter had been calling him about and was gone the next month. Pat was ready to take this over Murray's head when he was serendipitously contacted by the corporate office investigating Murray's leadership patterns. Fortunately for the project, Pat put it on a temporary hold, while he and Diane (Ralph's replacement) discussed how to rebuild it. After Murray's departure, Calvin addressed the project as one of his first orders of priority and set up failsafe methods that the goals and intentions of the error reporting project would be fully honored. Clear guidelines were established so that everyone knew the level of errors required before disciplinary action would take place.. And, since this level of errors was so unusual, and all agreed that someone with that pattern of errors should be disciplined, trust began to re-build in the program. Most importantly, leaders were supported in celebrating reporting of errors and having positive discussions around how they could be avoided in the future.

This story strongly illustrates the importance of trust for encouraging truth-telling, as well as how negative or punitive feedback can erode trust in a nanosecond! It takes a strong environment of trust to encourage and support such self-reporting and truth-telling.

What Kind of Environment Have You Created?

Now is a good time to step back, take a deep breath, and reflect for a moment on the environment you have created.

What have you done to build up, or to break down trust?

Have you displayed more of the characteristics of that best boss or worst boss that you recalled back at the beginning of Chapter 1 of this book?

What do you want to do moving forward? Whether it's leading a great project, successful team, or leaving a legacy of a career, what can you do differently in the future, starting today, to build those trusting relationships that set the foundation for exemplary performance? We believe that by making the *PACT*, through following the steps outlined in this book, you can do just that. And, in so doing, you will set your team members, your organization and yourself onto a new road of greatness that will take you places you never before imagined.

Chapter 9
THE FINAL CHAPTER

"The greatest glory in living lies not in never falling, but in rising every time we fall."

— *Melson Mandela*

Bringing it Together to
Start Your Own New Chapter

If you can put into practice the elements of the *PACT*, you will build such a strong, trusting, safe work environment, people will truly thrive. As you review the process, remember the following key points:

- *Begin by thinking about the qualities of the good bosses you have had.* They likely treated you with respect, dignity, fairness and honor. You should do the same with your employees.
- *Make your relationships "win-win-win."* Your success is dependent on your employees' success; you know it, and they should know it. Develop strategies that advance both parties' interests. Make the *PACT*! The organization's success is dependent on it too.

- *Where are you going, what do you want?* Understand what is important to your employees. It's not always obvious, and it's never simple. Find out what they need and help them get it.
- *Focus on being fair.* All employees should be treated fairly, but not all employees should be treated exactly the same. Each will have unique, personal needs and desires, and each should be considered as individuals. Don't try to create the same conditions for everyone, but work towards creating an environment free from animosity and jealousy.
- *Support and encourage more, critique less.* In a supervisory role you must expect a certain level of performance, but most of your employees will likely perform in at least a satisfactory way. Fulfill the requirements of your company as they relate to employee evaluation, but rather than harping on flaws and weaknesses, seek out ways to affirm the strengths and successes of your employees.
- *Share the big picture perspective.* Explain to your employees the company's strategy and tactics, and work to make the organizational culture explicit. These qualities of the organization should not be implicit or mysterious; they undoubtedly exist, so why not talk about them?
- *Clarify, clarify, clarify.* Don't allow your employees to "make stuff up"; when situations are unclear, you must make them clear. And...don't make stuff up yourself. Don't shy away from asking difficult questions.
- *Acknowledge successes.* In a genuine, specific way, acknowledge work well done by your employees. For some managers this may not come naturally; if

you are one of those, force yourself to do it. It will be worth it.

- *Provide regular feedback.* Your job is to support your employees, and to do that you must be in constant contact with them. Be constructive and helpful; don't let your employees' work go unnoticed.
- *Emphasize "playing well with others."* It begins in pre-school, and it never ends. Stress with your employees the importance of constructive collaboration; lead with a compelling vision; show them the benefits of working together, and transform their conflicts into experiences marked more by growth than tension.
- *Tell the truth.* Making the *PACT* will not work in an environment that does not have trust as its foundation. If your employees don't believe you, you cannot successfully lead them.

While making the *PACT* is straightforward and outlined in this book, it is far from easy. Some of what you have learned, particularly if you were trained by a "command and control" boss, you need to "unlearn." You must share how you feel with others; you must be vulnerable; you need to take risks, admit mistakes. You will have to accept messy desks, employees who leave work early (sometimes!) to see their children perform in a school play, and even—gasp!—employees who don't necessarily want to climb the corporate ladder. In the end, though, if you can focus on the fundamental tenets of the *PACT*, your employees will be more productive, more energized, and ultimately happier. When that happens...you will find that you will grow dramatically as a manager, a leader and a human being. And, the organization will grow to new heights!

Trust us.

Steps to Making and Keeping the *PACT*

Timing*	*PACT*'ing Step
Day 1	1. Setting the stage: My job is to support you in doing the best job you can do 2. Clarity of the specific job: a. Job description b. Position goals and expectations
Week 2	3. The bigger picture perspective: a. Share Team goals and expectations b. Share Organizational goals and expectations c. Discuss how their specific job fits in and contributes to this bigger picture 4. Preparing for the *PACT* discussion: a. Include a little "Get to know each other better" conversation, for example: • Ask about pivotal periods of the person's life, e.g. education/training choices, last job. • What contribution to your last job are you most proud of? b. Ask employee to be thinking about what they want from this job, both short-term and long-term, and that you'll discuss it during your next meeting.
Week 4	5. Initial exploration of employee's needs and aspirations: a. "In general, tell me a little about what's really important to you in a job?" b. "What about this job? What do you want to accomplish here?" Consider both short-term and long-term c. Clarify so that you are clear on the employees needs/aspirations 6. Make the initial *PACT*: a. Identify specific actions you can do to help support their goals/aspirations - make sure you can follow through on these actions b. Make an explicit agreement (*PACT*) that you will support each other's goals—meaning you support the employee's goals and the employee supports the organizational goals

* This is a relative time schedule. If you are conducting this with an existing employee you can typically go through all steps much more quickly. Make certain however, you even provide the most tenured employee some time to think between Step 4 and Step 5.

Timing	*PACT'*ing Step
Ongoing	7. Ongoing conversations: *Performance Support* process
Possible difficult situations	When there are challenges: • Explore past experiences and possible lessons to be gained from them: "What difficulties did you encounter in you past jobs?" • If an employee requests support that you are having trouble understanding or coming up with a reasonable way in which you can support, ask: "Tell me what you think I could do to support you here" or "What would my support look like here?" • Practice the *Conflict Transformation* process when needed.
Personal Develop-ment to be more skilled as a *PACT'*ing boss	• Self-reflection • Feedback—360 and/or other authentic input from others • Find a coach and/or a mentor • Honing your skills to effectively practice the People*PACT* Principles of Humane Leadership

CONFLICT TRANSFORMATION MODEL©
PREPARING FOR THE CONVERSATION
Worksheet

Completing this worksheet in advance can help your prepare for a productive and possibly transformational conversation.

1. INTENTION	
Before you start, check out your intention to ensure it is trustworthy.	
Process Step	*Comments*
Think about your intention for bringing up the issue— what is it?	
Does your intention align with the vision/goals/values of the team? How?	
Do you have an underlying agenda that could possibly be an obstacle to resolution? What might it be?	

2. Preparing to *Open the Door for Dialogue: Stating the Issue*	
Process Step	*Draft Statements*
How can you state the issue without blame, judgment, attack or defense? Remember: keep them safe and open up your vulnerability.	

3. Recognize your contribution to the issue/problem	
Process Step	*Comments or Draft Statements*
Consider what you might have misinterpreted, not done, mis-communicated, etc.	

the People*PACT*®

4. Outline issue objectively—with specific example	
Process Step	*Comments or Draft Statements*
What are the objective data/facts?	

5. Identify what is at stake—relative to the vision/relationship	
Process Step	*Comments or Draft Statements*
Reinforce your intention here and the big picture perspective	

6. Consider possible solutions	
Process Step	*Comments or Draft Statements*
While considering possible solutions, keep in mind there may be others you are not thinking of…be open to your partner having additional ideas.	
Craft your request—if applicable	

Examples of Statements for Conflict Transformation Dialogue

POSSIBLE STATEMENTS	
PROCESS STEP	**DRAFT STATEMENTS**
State the issue.	I worry about our ability to meet deadlines.
Outline Issue: Select a specific example that illustrates the situation. Use objective data.	Last month we missed two dead-lines.......*name*...and had to negotiate extensions.
Remember to keep them safe and put yourself as vulnerable.	I know you have a lot on your plate right now. I have been remiss in bringing this up before today.
Identify your contribution to the problem.	I've been concerned about the missed deadlines for some time now, yet been avoiding talking with you about it.
Clarify what is at stake. *Include your intention.*	I'm concerned that if we don't take an active role in fixing the deadline issue, we will fall further behind and not meet expectations with our partners in other areas. Our relationship is important to me. I feel I may risk our relationship by bringing this up to you.
Indicate your wish to resolve the issue.	I'm committed to helping resolve this issue.

References

Arrien, A. (1993). *The four-fold way.* San Francisco: Harper.

Berry, L. (1999). *Discovering the soul of service: The nine drivers of sustainable business success.* New York: The Free Press.

Branham, L. (2005). *The 7 hidden reasons employees leave: How to read the subtle signs and act before it's too late.* New York: AMACOM Books.

Buckingham, M., & Coffman, C. (1999) *First: Break all the rules.* New York: Simon and Schuster.

Buckingham, M., & Clifton, D. (2001). *Now, discover your strengths.* New York: Free Press.

Covey. S. (2004). *The 8ᵗʰ Habit: From effectiveness to greatness.* New York: Free Press.

Drexler, A., Sibbet, D., & Forrester, R., (1988). *Team Building: Blueprints for Productivity and Satisfaction.* San Diego, CA: NTL Institute for Applied Behavioral Science and University Associates.

Goleman, D. (1995). *Emotional intelligence: Why it can matter more than IQ?* New York: Bantam Books.

Goleman, D., Boyatzis, R., & McKee, A. (2002). *Primal Leadership: Learning to Lead with Emotional Intelligence.* Harvard Business School Press.

Goleman, D. (1998, November-December). "What makes a leader?" *Harvard Business Review*, 92-102.

Grimaldi, L. (2000, December). "If bosses motivate, workers stay." *Meetings & Conventions*, 35 (13), 26.

Reina, D., & Reina, M. (1999). *Trust & betrayal in the workplace.* San Francisco: Berrett-Koehler.

Rosner, B., Halcrow, A., & Levins, A. (2001). *The bosses' survival guide.* Columbus, OH: McGraw-Hill.

Scott, S. (2002). *Fierce conversations: Achieving success at work and in life once conversation at a time.* New York: Viking.

Wilson, L., & Wilson, H. (1998). *Play to win! Choosing growth over fear in work and life.* Austin, TX: Bard Press.

Zemke, R. (2000, February). "Can you manage trust?" *Training*, 37(2), 76-83.

To Learn More About Making the *PACT*

*i*BossWell, Inc. is our strategic partner in delivering consulting support to organizations seeking to advance their leadership and *PACT*'ing skills. *i*BossWell is a leadership and organizational development company, working with not-for-profits, for-profits and government agencies to bring success through building greater alignment between *vision*, *tactics* and *organizational culture*.

Their integrated approach includes planning facilitation, assessment, consulting, workshops, executive coaching and board training to help lead organizations to the next level of excellence. *i*BossWell is the exclusive provider for the People*PACT* process approach to exemplary performance.

The PeoplePACT author, Denise McNerney, is CEO of *i*BossWell, Inc.
For further information contact:
*i*BossWell, Inc.
913-642-1416 - Midwest Office
808-214-9809 - Hawaii/Pacific Rim Office
Email: coach@ibosswell.com
Web address: www.ibosswell.com

Also, check out our website: www.People*PACT*.com for ongoing new information regarding practicing the *PACT*'ing process.